Discover

OXFORD

Undoubtedly the best way to explore and discover Oxford is on foot. The city is relatively flat, many of the important buildings are difficult or impossible to reach by car, and walking not only enables the visitor to admire them but also to soak up the unique atmosphere of this university city.

But where to walk especially when time may be limited?

This book of circular walks aims to answer that question. The walks all start and finish either in the centre of the city or close to it. Most are less than two miles long, some less than one mile. All include several colleges and other significant buildings along the route.

The aim of the book is to enable the visitor to sightsee Oxford and in particular the university and college buildings in an easy and structured way. The walk directions are clear, straightforward and not encumbered by lengthy detail. A section at the end of each walk gives thumbnail comments on the main buildings on the route but does not aim to be a definitive source of information. There are many other publications which do this.

So enjoy your time in Oxford. Take a short walk or three and, with the help of this book, hopefully your pleasure and knowledge will be increased.

TOWN AND COUNTRY WALKS IN OXFORD

5. Outside the Medieval City   1½ miles   *page 39*

Colleges   St John's, Keble, Trinity, Wadham, New, Magdalen, The Queen's, St Edmund Hall

Other buildings   Martyrs Memorial, Taylor Institute, Ashmolean Museum, Lamb and Flag, Eagle and Child, University Museum, Rhodes House, King's Arms, New Bodleian Library, Holywell Music Room, Examination Schools, St Peter-in-the-East, Bridge of Sighs, Turf Tavern

6. Old and New   1 mile   *page 49*

Colleges   St Peter's, Nuffield, Worcester

Other buildings   St Mary Magdalen, St Michael's at the Northgate, Oxford Union Society, Wesley Memorial Church, Oxford Castle, Canal, Beaumont Palace

7. Urban and Rural Oxford   2½ or 3½ miles   *page 57*

Colleges   New, Harris Manchester, Mansfield, Linacre, Keble, Trinity, Wadham

Other buildings   Sheldonian Theatre, King's Arms, Holywell Music Room, School of Pathology, University Cricket Ground, Rhodes House, New Bodleian Library

8. Jericho   2 miles   *page 65*

Colleges   Worcester, Kellogg, Nuffield

Other buildings   Beaumont Palace, Rewley House, Oxford University Press, Synagogue, St Barnabas, Canal, Isis Lock

9. Aspects of Oxford   5 miles   *page 73*

Colleges   Christ Church, Pembroke, Magdalen, Keble, Trinity, Wadham, Hertford, Brasenose, All Souls

Other buildings   Town Hall, War Memorial Garden, Christ Church Meadow, Botanic Garden, Magdalen Bridge, Victoria Fountain, St Clement's, Rhodes House, New Bodleian Library, Sheldonian Theatre, Divinity School, Clarendon Building, Bridge of Sighs, Schools Quad, Bodleian Library, Radcliffe Camera, St Mary the Virgin

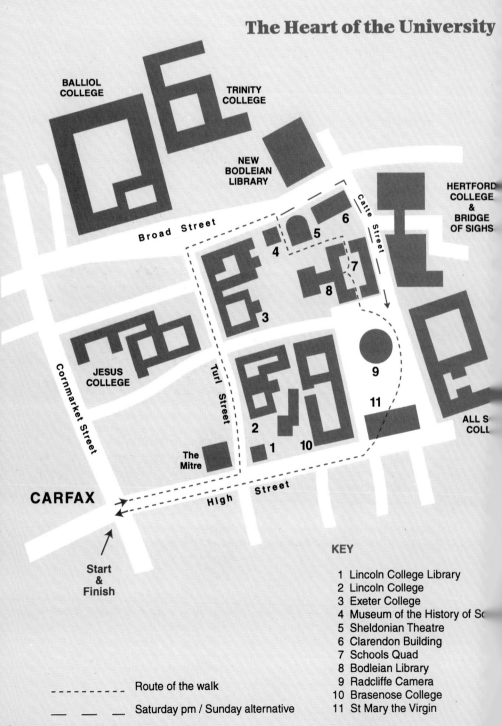

BALLIOL COLLEGE

TRINITY COLLEGE

NEW BODLEIAN LIBRARY

HERTFORD COLLEGE & BRIDGE OF SIGHS

Broad Street

Catte Street

6

5

4

7

8

3

Cornmarket Street

JESUS COLLEGE

Turl Street

9

11

2

1   10

The Mitre

ALL S COLL

CARFAX

High Street

Start & Finish

KEY

1 Lincoln College Library
2 Lincoln College
3 Exeter College
4 Museum of the History of S
5 Sheldonian Theatre
6 Clarendon Building
7 Schools Quad
8 Bodleian Library
9 Radcliffe Camera
10 Brasenose College
11 St Mary the Virgin

- - - - - - - Route of the walk

— — — Saturday pm / Sunday alternative

Walk 1
THE HEART OF THE UNIVERSITY

Introduction
This walk takes in some of the most stunning and well known buildings in Oxford. Traffic restrictions over much of the route happily ensure the walk is pleasant, safe and relaxed - ideal conditions for appreciating the buildings and soaking up the atmosphere they generate. If you only do one walk in Oxford this is the one you should do - and remember to take a camera!

Length
Although the distance covered is only a little over half a mile you should allow at least 30 minutes. This is a walk for pausing, for looking in awe and for marvelling at man's ability to create, over several centuries, buildings which wonderfully complement each other and together create an ambience felt possibly nowhere else in the world.

Saturday pm and Sunday Alternative
Access to some areas is restricted on Saturday afternoons and Sundays and because of this an alternative route is given for part of this walk. There is no difference either in the length of the walk or in the time required to complete it.

Buildings
To ensure directions are clear and straightforward minimal information is included in the walk description on the buildings seen. However, the 'Additional Information' section on *pages 10-13* provides a brief overview of each of the locations printed in **bold type**.

Starting Point
This circular walk starts and finishes at Carfax in the centre of Oxford.

The Walk

All Souls College skyline

From Carfax, with your back to Carfax Tower, walk away from the tower along the High Street, passing three entrances to the Covered Market, until you reach **The Mitre**.

Students in 'sub fusc'

Turn left into Turl Street which gets its name from a twirling gate in the city wall situated, until its demolition in 1722, at the far end of the street. **Lincoln College Library** is on your right as you turn and the street also contains three colleges. Walk down Turl Street passing first **Lincoln College** on the right. This college, founded in 1427 by Robert Fleming Bishop of Lincoln remains, despite many alterations over the centuries, one of the least spoilt legacies of medieval Oxford. On the left, beyond Market Street, is **Jesus College** the only college founded during the reign of Elizabeth I and opposite on the right is **Exeter College** whose founder, Walter de Stapleton, has the dubious distinction of being the only founder of an Oxford College to be murdered.

As you approach the end of Turl Street the front quad of **Trinity College** with its gate tower in the background is visible across Broad Street through the 1737 wrought iron gates. To the left of Trinity is **Balliol College**.

At the end of Turl Street turn right into Broad Street. After 100 yards you will find on your right the **Museum of the History of Science** which occupies the building of the original Ashmolean Museum, the first British public museum.

On Saturday afternoons and Sundays skip the next page and a half and go to the section of the walk description headed 'Saturday pm and Sunday Alternative' on page 8

Just beyond the Museum go right through a small archway and keep right with the **Sheldonian Theatre** designed by Christopher Wren on your left to arrive in a courtyard with the Sheldonian on your left and the 15th century **Divinity School** on your right.

Continue to an open gravelled courtyard with, on your left, the **Clarendon Building** with its rooftop statues representing the nine muses, and visible ahead across the road, the **Bridge of Sighs** linking the two buildings of **Hertford College**.

Bridge of Sighs

Turn right opposite the Clarendon through an opening which leads to **Schools Quad** now part of the **Bodleian Library** but originally built as lecture rooms and libraries.

Through the door behind the statue of the Earl of Pembroke enter the Divinity School.

On leaving the Divinity School exit Schools Quad on the right between the 'Schola Musicae' and the 'Schola Naturalis Philosophiae' to the stunning Radcliffe Square. Directly ahead dominating the square is the **Radcliffe Camera** with its original ground floor arcade now enclosed to form part of the building; to the right is **Brasenose College** and to the left **All Souls College**.

Sundial - All Souls College

Walk to the left keeping the Radcliffe Camera on your right and take a moment to look through the gates at the Great Quad of All Souls designed by Nicholas Hawksmoor and built in the first quarter of the 18th century. On the north side is a sundial designed by Christopher Wren when he was the college bursar.

Ahead is the university church of **St Mary the Virgin**. For a small charge it is possible to climb the 127 steps of the tower and to be rewarded with probably the most breathtaking views of anywhere in Oxford.

Enter St Mary the Virgin through the tower door and walk through the gift shop into the church. Exit diagonally opposite at the back of the church into the High Street facing the north side of Oriel College with a statue of Cecil Rhodes towards the top of the tower. This is the only statue in Oxford of a man dressed in civilian as opposed to clerical or military clothes.

Looking towards Radcliffe Square

Turn right and walk along The High, past Brasenose College on the right, to the finishing point at Carfax.

Saturday pm and Sunday Alternative

Continue along Broad Street to the traffic lights passing on your right first the **Sheldonian Theatre,** designed by Christopher Wren, and then the **Clarendon Building** and its rooftop statues representing the nine muses. On your left is the **New Bodleian Library**.

8

At the traffic lights turn right into Catte Street and after a few yards on the left is the **Bridge of Sighs** linking the two buildings of **Hertford College**. On the right the Sheldonian and the Clarendon can be seen from a different perspective.

A few yards further, opposite the main entrance to Hertford College, is the entrance to **Schools Quad** now part of the **Bodleian Library** but originally built as lecture rooms and libraries. The crests on the entrance doors are of the 20 colleges in existence in 1620 when the Quad was built.

Continue down Catte Street to reach the stunning Radcliffe Square. Directly ahead dominating the square is the **Radcliffe Camera** with its original ground floor arcade now enclosed to form part of the building; to the right is **Brasenose College** and to the left **All Souls College**.

Clarendon Building

St Mary the Virgin from High Street

Walk to the left keeping the Radcliffe Camera on your right and take a moment to look through the gates at the Great Quad of All Souls designed by Nicholas Hawksmoor and built in the first quarter of the 18th century. On the north side is a sundial designed by Christopher Wren when he was the college bursar. Ahead is the university church of **St Mary the Virgin**. For a small charge it is possible to climb the 127 steps of the tower and to be rewarded with probably the most breathtaking views of anywhere in Oxford.

Enter St Mary the Virgin through the tower door and walk through the gift shop into the church. Exit diagonally opposite at the back of the church into the High Street facing the north side of Oriel College with a statue of Cecil Rhodes towards the top of the tower. This is the only statue in Oxford of a man dressed in civilian as opposed to clerical or military clothes.

Turn right and walk along The High, past Brasenose College on the right, to the finishing point at Carfax.

Additional Information

The Mitre
Once a famous Inn with a history going back to around 1300 the present building dates mainly from about 1630 although the original 13th century cellar survives. The upper floors have been converted into student rooms.

Lincoln College Library
Dating from 1709 the former All Saints' Church is now the library of Lincoln College.

Lincoln College
The college had a precarious financial existence in its early years and was close to extinction on at least two occasions. However, new statutes in 1479 and further benefactions in the 15th and 16th centuries eased the situation. Notable Fellows of the college include John Wesley the evangelist and founder of Methodism, Lord Florey who developed penicillin and the philosopher Samuel Alexander, one of the first Jews to be elected to an Oxford fellowship (1882-93).

Jesus College

Jesus College
Founded in 1571 by Hugh Price although, when approached by him for her support on the project, Elizabeth I claimed the title of foundress. Price was Treasurer of St David's Cathedral in Wales and for centuries the college gave preference to candidates from Wales. Even today St. David's day is celebrated with a Welsh service in the chapel. In 1974 Jesus was among the first group of men's colleges to admit women. Notable former students include T.E. Lawrence (Lawrence of Arabia) and ex Prime Minister Harold Wilson.

Exeter College

Exeter College
In the 19th century the college was at the forefront of Oxford sport being amongst the earliest to promote rowing and to have it's own cricket ground. In 1850 it organised the inaugural university athletics meeting and this tradition reached a pleasing climax when in 1954 an undergraduate of the college, Roger Bannister, became the first person in the world to run a mile in less than 4 minutes.

Trinity College

(see also walks 5 and 7, pages 45 and 63)
Built on the site of Durham College the 13th century Benedictine priory, Trinity, founded in 1555 by Sir Thomas Pope, was the first college to be founded by a layman. Undergraduates of the college include William Pitt and the Earl of Guildford who both subsequently became Prime Minister. Under Pitt's administration America was colonised and in 1776 under Guildford's, who by then had become Lord North, it was lost.

Trinity College Broad St Gates

Balliol College

John de Balliol, a powerful northern nobleman, insulted the Bishop of Durham and as part of his penance was required to found and maintain a place of learning in Oxford for poor scholars. In 1263 he rented a house for this purpose which later became Balliol College. Balliol is one of three colleges claiming to be the oldest in Oxford and bases its claim on the fact that its members have lived communally on this site since 1263 (the other two claimants are Merton and University).

Museum of the History of Science

The building was opened in 1683 as the Ashmolean Museum, but was also used for lectures and, in the basement, as a chemical laboratory. Amongst the many exhibits are the Lewis Evans collection of scientific instruments, an extremely important collection of early astronomical and mathematical instruments, and the blackboard, together with his calculations, used by Einstein when he lectured in Oxford on the theory of relativity.

Sheldonian Theatre

(see also walk 7 page 60)
Built 1664-69 this is the first major building designed by Sir Christopher Wren who at the time was a 31 year old Professor of Astronomy! The design is based on the Marcellus Theatre in Rome and the theatre is named after Archbishop Sheldon, University Chancellor and Archbishop of Canterbury, who footed the bill. The 'Emperors Heads' on the Broad Street side of the building simply mark the northern boundary and, although visually attractive, are of no other significance.

Sheldonian Theatre

Divinity School

This is the oldest university as opposed to college building in Oxford. Built 1420-1483 the initials or coat of arms of those who contributed to the cost are carved on the bosses of the magnificent ceiling. Initially the building was for Divinity lectures and examinations but it now forms part of the Bodleian Library.

Clarendon Building *(see also walk 8 Oxford University Press, page 70)*

Designed by Nicholas Hawksmoor, a pupil of Wren, and built in 1712 by the Oxford University Press for their printing works which had outgrown previous premises in the Sheldonian Theatre. The building is now part of the Bodleian Library and the Press is in modern buildings a mile away. However, a felicitous reminder of its former activities is the 'Clarendon Press' imprint on all OUP books.

Bridge of Sighs *(see also walk 5 page 47)*

One of the most frequently photographed and well known landmarks in Oxford and familiarly named after the Ponte dei Sospiri in Venice. The bridge, built 1913-14, links the two buildings of Hertford College.

Hertford College

Hertford has had a very chequered and unusual existence. Its history goes back to the foundation of Hart Hall in 1284 and during the next 600 years, culminating in its refoundation in 1874, it was twice an academic hall and twice a college. Evelyn Waugh, an undergraduate here, portrayed Oxford life in the 1920's as he saw it in his novel 'Brideshead Revisited' a portrait of an Oxford now long gone.

Schools Quad - James I

Schools Quad

'Schools' in this context means 'teaching rooms' and the quad was built 1613-24 to bring together the lecture rooms which until then were dispersed throughout the city. Teaching in those days was in Latin and over the doors, in Latin, can still be seen the early 17th century curriculum. The statue is of the 3rd Earl of Pembroke, Chancellor of the University when the quad was built and the man to whom Shakespeare dedicated his first folio. Schools Quad is now part of the Bodleian Library.

Bodleian Library

The main research library of the University, founded by Sir Thomas Bodley and opened in 1602. Today it is housed in several buildings and contains nearly seven million books, more than one million maps and has more than 160 kilometres of shelving. It is not a lending library and even Charles I, when he was resident in Oxford during the Civil War, was refused permission to borrow a book.

Radcliffe Camera

John Radcliffe who studied at Oxford and later became physician to the joint monarchs William and Mary left much of his wealth and all of his medical books to the university. More than 20 years later in 1737, after the site had finally been cleared, building work started on this first round library in Britain. In 1860 it became part of the Bodleian Library and is now reading rooms mainly used by undergraduates.

Radcliffe Camera

Brasenose College *(see also walk 3 page 28)*

Founded in 1509 and named after the 'brazen nose' 13th century door-knocker which students took with them to Stamford in Lincolnshire in 1333 when they left the then turbulent situation in Oxford for a calmer environment. In 1890 the college bought a complete house so they could get the knocker back! It now has prime position above the Principle's place at High Table.

All Souls College *(see also walk 3 page 28)*

A unique college which takes neither undergraduate nor graduate students, only research Fellows. The first female Fellow, Susan Hurley of Santa Barbara, California was elected in 1981. Founded in 1438 as a memorial to those who died in the 100 Years War with France its full name is The College of All Souls of the Faithful Departed.

Great Quad - All Souls

St Mary the Virgin *(see also walk 3 page 28)*

Although mentioned in the Domesday Book of 1086 the oldest parts of the church we now see the last in a series built on the same site, are the 13th century tower and 14th century spire. The university developed in the area of the church and until specialised university buildings were available, St Mary's was used for university meetings, examinations and ceremonies. Indeed the flat roofed extension, now a café, was once the university parliament building.

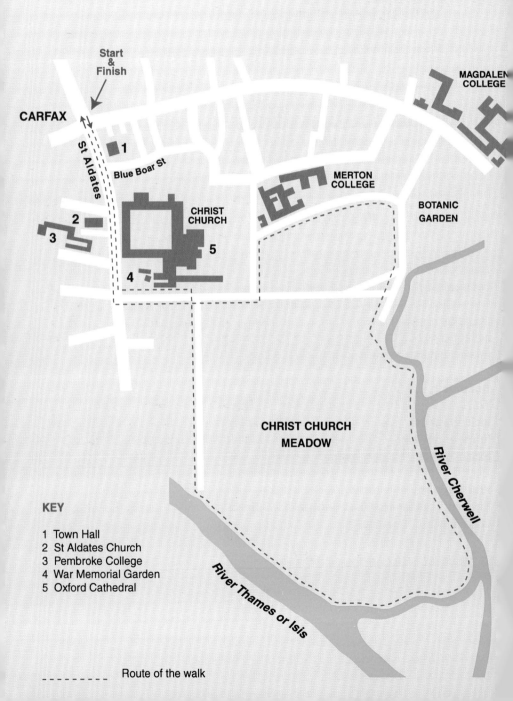

Start
&
Finish

CARFAX

St Aldates

1

Blue Boar St

MAGDALEN
COLLEGE

MERTON
COLLEGE

BOTANIC
GARDEN

CHRIST
CHURCH

2

3

5

4

CHRIST CHURCH
MEADOW

River Cherwell

KEY

1 Town Hall
2 St Aldates Church
3 Pembroke College
4 War Memorial Garden
5 Oxford Cathedral

River Thames or Isis

– – – – – – –   Route of the walk

Walk 2
CHRIST CHURCH MEADOW

Introduction

This delightful walk through meadows and along river banks is within very easy reach of the city centre. There are many picturesque spots along the route ideal for picnics or just for sitting and relaxing. If you want to get away from the hustle and bustle of the city, or to see a very different Oxford, try this walk. It is easy walking and with the exception of 6 steps which can be avoided, completely flat.

Length

The full length is two miles but the time taken to complete it will vary. Normal walking pace will take about 1 hour but this walk is made for strolling and it would be wiser perhaps to allow a little longer. Of course any time spent picnicking or simply sitting and relaxing should be added to these timings.

Alternative Route To Avoid 6 Steps

Soon after the start there are 6 steps in the War Memorial Garden and an alternative route is given for this small section of the walk for those who wish to avoid the steps. The alternative does not affect either the length of the walk or the time required to complete it.

Buildings

To ensure directions are clear and straightforward minimal information is included in the walk description on the buildings seen. However, the 'Additional Information' section on *pages 19-21* provides a brief overview of each of the locations printed in **bold type**.

Starting Point

The starting and finishing point for this circular walk is Carfax in the middle of Oxford.

The Walk

Museum of Oxford

From Carfax walk south down the left hand side of St Aldates passing after a few yards the **Town Hall** and the Museum of Oxford, with **Tom Tower** the imposing bell tower of **Christ Church** clearly visible ahead. A little further, as you pass Christ Church, notice the cardinals' hats carved on the towers, a reminder of the college's founder, Cardinal Wolsey. Also look through the main gate of Christ Church at Tom Quad, the largest quad in Oxford, with a lead copy of Giovanni da Bologna's *Mercury* in the centre. Across the road on the right is **Pembroke College** with its entrance tucked away beyond St Aldate's church.

To avoid 6 steps in the War Memorial Garden skip the rest of this page and go to the paragraph on the next page headed 'Alternative Route To Avoid 6 Steps'

Continue past a garage entrance and about 100 yards after Christ Church turn left through imposing wrought iron gates into the **War Memorial Garden**. Notice the sword inlaid into the paving at the entrance with an inscription from John Bunyan's *Pilgrims Progress* 'My sword I give to him that shall succeed me in my pilgrimage'.

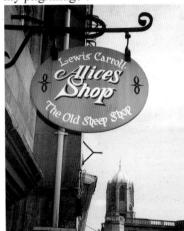

The Old Sheep Shop

Walk 5 or 6 paces into the Garden and pause to look at some of the buildings. On the left is Christ Church with Tom Tower and the Hall in full view, on the right is the north wing of the Faculty of Music containing the Bate Collection of English and European woodwind, brass and percussion instruments. Behind, across the road, is Alice's Shop where Alice of *Alice in Wonderland* and *Alice through the Looking Glass* bought her sweets. Alice in real life was Alice Liddell the daughter of the Dean of Christ Church.

Walk through the Garden, up two sets of three steps each, into **Christ Church Meadow**.

Alternative Route To Avoid 6 Steps

Immediately after Christ Church there is an entrance on the left with a notice *Entrance to Garages Do Not Obstruct.* Turn left through this entrance and after 100 yards turn left again. After a further 50 yards rejoin the main walk opposite the visitors entrance to Christ Church.

The diversion to avoid the steps rejoins the main walk at this point.

After a few yards, opposite the visitors entrance to Christ Church, turn right along Poplar Walk which was planted in 1872 by Alice's father Dean Liddell. Continue between the trees, along this very pleasant stretch of meadow which often has contented cattle grazing on your left, and after a quarter of a mile reach the River Thames or Isis as it is known hereabouts.

Turn left and walk along the side of the river stopping if you wish to sit and refresh mind, body or both, at one of the many convenient benches along the way.

After 300 yards ignore the bridge on your right and continue straight ahead keeping to the pathway. The walk now follows a delightful, slow running link between the two rivers of Oxford, the Isis and the Cherwell, a little known but idyllic stretch of water for **punting**.

A further half mile brings you to a fork in the river and the pathway follows the left fork. Clearly visible over to the right, behind the trees, is **Magdalen College** Tower where from the top at dawn every May Day morning the choir sings an invocation to summer whilst several thousand people dance and make merry in the street below.

Keep to the path and after another 200 yards ignore the major path, Broad Walk, on your left and keep right reaching after a further 100 yards the railings of the **Botanic Garden** on your right.

Magdalen College Tower

After a few yards you will reach a fork with the exit gates from the Meadow straight ahead and some cottages on the left. Do not go through the gates but turn left keeping Meadow Cottages on your right. Notice the plaque set into the wall commemorating the feat of **James Sadler**, the first English aeronaut, who made a successful ascent in a balloon close to here in 1784 landing six miles away near the small village of Woodeaton.

Soon after the cottages and other buildings the path follows alongside the ancient **city wall** behind which is Merton College Fellows Garden, with further ahead **Merton College**, one of three colleges which claim to be the oldest in Oxford.

At the end of Merton College the path turns sharp left. Turn left with the path keeping the sports field of Christ Church Choir School on your left and after 30 yards look through the gate on the right for a superb view of **Oxford Cathedral,** one of the smallest cathedrals in England.

Continue for another 50 yards to reach Broad Walk and turn right with the south side of Christ Church on your right. After a few yards pass Popular Walk to reach and walk through the Memorial Garden (or veer right to take the diversion avoiding the steps) and arrive once again in St Aldates.

Turn right to retrace your steps to Carfax and to the finish of the walk.

Additional Information

Town Hall
Opened by the Prince of Wales, later Edward VII, on 12 May 1897. The results of parliamentary elections are announced from the balcony over the entrance. On the roof is a weather vane featuring a golden ox from the city's coat-of-arms. On the south corner is the Museum of Oxford.

Tom Tower
Designed by Christopher Wren and built in 1682 above Wolsey's 1527 archway and turrets. Inside the tower is Great Tom, the loudest bell in Oxford, which chimes 101 times every evening at 9.05pm to recall the 101 students resident in 1682 and their curfew time of 9pm. However, as Great Tom keeps local time not GMT and since the city is 5 minutes west of Greenwich, the bell chimes at 9.05pm!

Tom Tower

Christ Church *(see also walk 3 page 26)*
Founded as Cardinal College in 1525 by Cardinal Wolsey but unfinished when he fell from power, the college was refounded as Christ Church in 1545 by Henry VIII. Perhaps the grandest of Oxford colleges it numbers amongst its alumnae 14 Prime Ministers, John Wesley the founder of Methodism, and William Penn the founder of Pennsylvania. The college chapel is also the cathedral of the Oxford diocese.

Pembroke College
Founded in 1624 and named after the University Chancellor the 3rd Earl of Pembroke, the south side of the college incorporates a long stretch of the old city wall. Samuel Johnson, compiler of the dictionary and an undergraduate at Pembroke, complained when fined for skipping a lecture that he had 'been fined tuppence for missing a lecture that was not worth a penny'. Another student James Smithson left his fortune to the United States government who used it to found the Smithsonian Institute.

Pembroke College

War Memorial Garden
Laid out in 1925 the garden commemorates all Oxford people, whether from the city or the university, who died in the First World War.

Christ Church Meadow

Part of the meadow was a gift from Lady Montacute who in 1454 was buried in the priory of St Frideswide: the priory was subsequently incorporated into the college chapel during the building of Christ Church. It is difficult to believe that during the 1950's and 1960's various schemes were put forward to build a road through the meadow and only intense opposition resulted in the plans finally being shelved in 1966.

Memorial Garden Gates

Punting

The word 'punt' first appeared in written English about AD1000 and meant any small craft. Nowadays it is a long, narrow, flat bottomed boat propelled by pushing a pole against the bottom of the river. Sounds simple but watching some people's attempts can be an enjoyable and hilarious experience!

Magdalen College *(see also walk 5 page 46)*

Pronounced 'Maudlin' and founded by William of Waynflete during the Wars of the Roses in 1458, it has 100 acres of grounds, more than a mile of riverside walks and a herd of deer. The 144 ft high tower was used as an observation post during the Civil War and was stocked with missiles to be used if Cromwell's forces attempted to march over the bridge. Edward Gibbon of *Decline & Fall of the Roman Empire* fame described his 14 months here as 'the most idle and unprofitable of my whole life'.

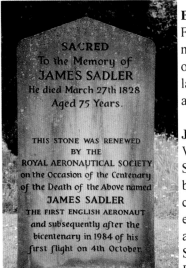

Gravestone - James Sadler (in the churchyard)

Botanic Garden

Founded in 1621 as a Physic Garden to provide medicinal herbs, it has evolved into a collection of over 8,000 plants in a compact, beautifully laid out setting accurately reflecting the appearance of a Tudor or Stuart college garden.

James Sadler

Whilst working as a laboratory technician Sadler constructed a 170 feet circumference balloon and on 4th October 1784 before a great crowd he 'ascended into the Atmosphere' to an estimated height of 3,600 feet and travelled about 6 miles. He is buried in the churchyard of St Peter-in-the-East which is now part of St Edmund Hall.

Christ Church from the Meadow

City Wall *(see also introduction to walk 5 on page 39).*
The construction date of Oxford's first city wall is generally reckoned to be 911. Over the following centuries the wall was periodically destroyed, rebuilt, improved, moved and strengthened. This part of the wall is Norman and dates from around 1080.

Merton College *(see also walk 3 page 27)*
Founded in 1264 the college is one of three which claim to be the oldest in Oxford (the others are Balliol and University). Its statutes were a model not only for all other Oxford colleges for the next 150 years but also for Cambridge's first college, Peterhouse, which adopted Merton's statutes on its foundation in 1284. A former Warden (Head) of Merton, William Harvey, discovered the circulation of the blood.

Oxford Cathedral
Dates from 12th century and contains the reconstructed shrine of St Frideswide which was built in 1289 but destroyed in 1538 on Henry VIII's orders. Three of the original Priory bays were demolished by Cardinal Wolsey to make way for the quad thus helping to create one of the smallest cathedrals in England. It is the only church in the world to be both a cathedral and a college chapel.

Walk 3
13th Century Oxford

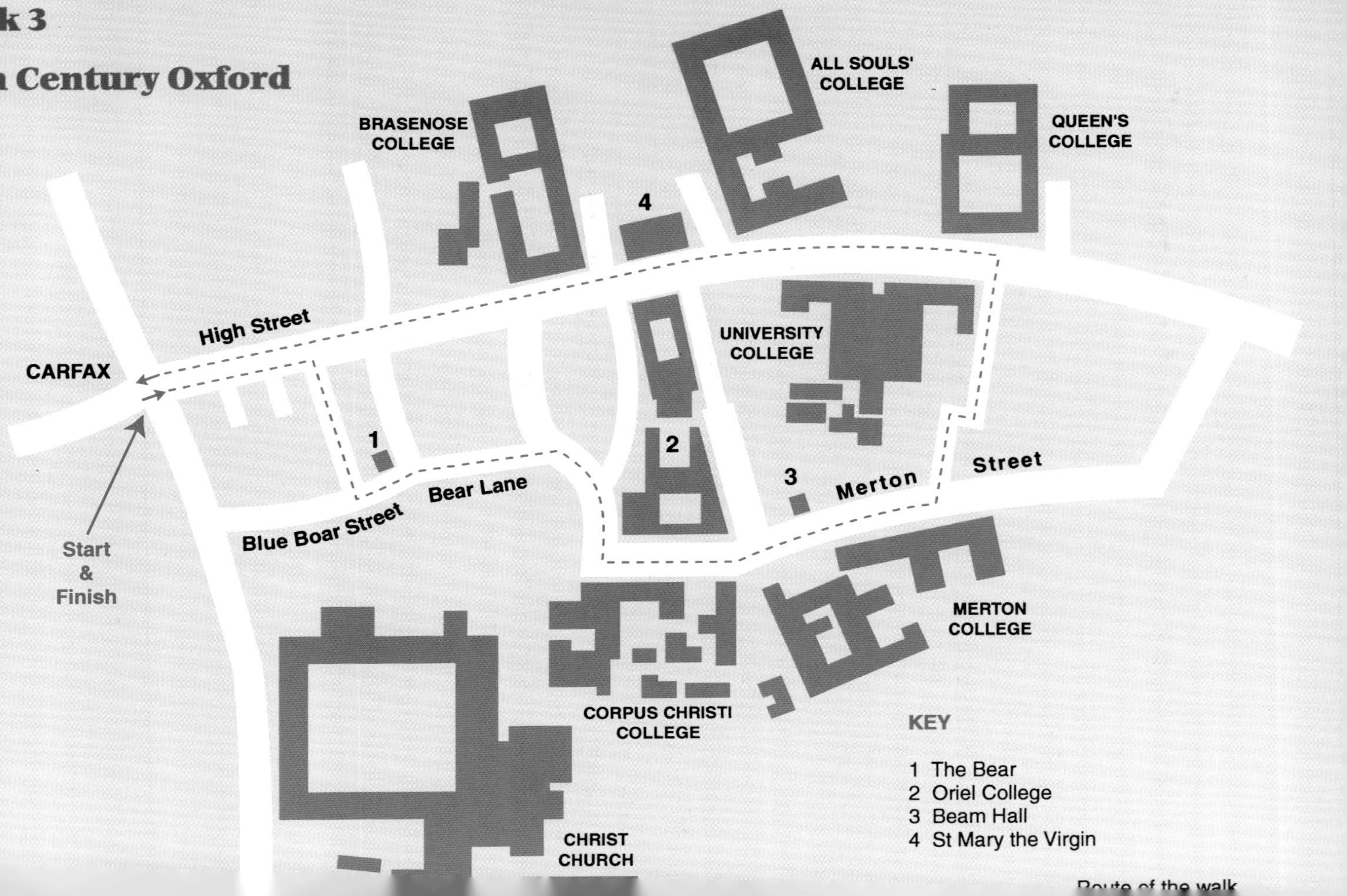

Route of the walk

QUEEN'S COLLEGE

ALL SOULS' COLLEGE

MERTON COLLEGE

Merton   Street

KEY

1 The Bear
2 Oriel College
3 Beam Hall
4 St Mary the Virgin

BRASENOSE COLLEGE

UNIVERSITY COLLEGE

CORPUS CHRISTI COLLEGE

CHRIST CHURCH

High Street

Bear Lane

Blue Boar Street

CARFAX

Start & Finish

Walk 3
13th Century Oxford

Introduction

University and Merton colleges, two of the three colleges claiming to be the oldest in Oxford, are on the route of this walk as is the church of St Mary the Virgin which, in the days before there were specialised university buildings, was used for examinations and major university ceremonies including conferment of degrees. Six other colleges, a building which in medieval times was an academic hall, and a pub with its origins in the 14th century are also on the walk. Altogether a step back into the early days of Oxford and the university.

Length

This short, flat walk of three quarters of a mile can be completed in 30 minutes. Although it is all within the old city boundary you will find it, except for the High Street, very peaceful and relaxing.

Buildings

To ensure directions are clear and straightforward minimal information is included in the walk description on the buildings seen. However, the 'Additional Information' section on *pages 26-28* provides a brief overview of each of the locations printed in **bold type**.

Starting Point

The walk, which is circular, starts and finishes in the centre of Oxford at Carfax.

The Walk

From Carfax Tower carefully cross to the St Aldates side of High Street, or 'the High' as it is commonly called, and walk along the right hand pavement.

After 100 yards, just before the traffic lights and opposite market entrance 3 turn right into a little alleyway called 'Wheatsheaf Yard'. This interesting alleyway is not only the home of one of the oldest firms of ironmongers in the country, **Gill & Co**, but, as almost the entire right hand side is a pub or brasserie, is also a good spot for eating and drinking.

Oriel College Houses

At the bottom of Wheatsheaf Yard turn left along Blue Boar passing on your left **The Bear** which has been in business in one form or another since 1247. Continue along Bear Lane to arrive in Oriel Square.

Bear right into Oriel Square passing several 18th century houses owned by Oriel College and used for accommodation. On your right is the eastern part of **Christ Church** and on your left **Oriel College** founded by Edward II in 1326, the fifth oldest college but the first to be founded by a monarch.

Walk to the bottom of Oriel Square and turn left into Merton Street passing **Corpus Christi College** on your right. If the entrance is open look through to see in the middle of Front Quad an elaborate sundial erected by Charles Turnbull in 1581. After a further 50 yards the wrought iron gates on the right lead to Christ Church Meadow but continue straight on beyond Magpie Lane. The building on the left immediately after Magpie Lane is accommodation for Corpus Christi students.

Merton College Tower

On the right is Merton College chapel and beyond is **Merton College** itself with its imposing gatehouse tower and statues of the founder, Walter de Merton; the king at the time, Henry III; and between St John the Baptist and various animals.

Across the road from Merton is **Beam Hall** now owned by Merton and used for seminar and computing rooms. Continue along Merton Street and after a few yards on the left is a gateway which leads to a Real Tennis court. Real Tennis has been played in Oxford for more than 500 years and this court is the second oldest still in play in England (the oldest is at Hampton Court).

After another few yards turn left up University College bridleway and through the wrought iron gates. The modern building on the right after the dogleg is accommodation for first year Univ students.

Emerging onto the High Street immediately opposite is **The Queen's College** with its distinctive cupola and statue of Queen Caroline the wife of George II. Turn left along the High Street with **University College** on the left. The main entrance to the college is reached after 50 yards and a few yards further on notice the wall plaque referring to Robert Boyle and Robert Hooker.

Cupola - The Queen's College

Just beyond and across the road is **All Souls College** with, on the entrance tower, a relief of the Resurrection of the Dead above statues of the founder, Henry Chichele Archbishop of Canterbury and of Henry VI. Immediately after Catte Street is **St Mary the Virgin** the parish church of the university.

On the left just after Magpie Lane is the northern wing of Oriel College. Named the 'Rhodes Building' after Cecil Rhodes, an Oriel graduate, benefactor and founder of Rhodes Scholarships. His statue at the top of the entrance tower is the only one in Oxford of a man in civilian as opposed to clerical or military dress.

A few yards further but across the road is the High Street frontage of **Brasenose College** with its eight oriel windows. Despite appearances the main entrance to Brasenose is not on the High but in Radcliffe Square.

Carfax Tower and the end of the walk is now in sight just a little way along the High.

Brasenose College

25

Additional Information

Gill & Co

Founded in 1530 by the Smythe family this is one of the oldest firms of ironmongers in the country. The firm changed its name several times over the succeeding centuries finally becoming Gill & Co in 1922. Well known to Oxford people it stocks over 9,000 items and 'try Gills' is a frequently heard piece of advice.

The Bear

The Bear

Originally stretching to the High Street and known as Parne Hall it was burnt down in 1421, rebuilt as Le Tabard, renamed 'The Bear' in 1432 and by the mid 16th century was one of the main taverns in Oxford. Later it became a coaching inn with 30 rooms, stabling for 30 horses and a tavern on the site of the present pub. When the coaching inn closed in 1801 the tavern was renamed The Bear.

Christ Church *(see also walk 2 page 19)*

The medieval university included five colleges founded by religious orders to revive monastic learning. During the Dissolution of the Monasteries one of these, Canterbury College, a Benedictine foundation exclusively for monks from Canterbury Cathedral Priory was incorporated into Christ Church. Although nothing remains of the original buildings the gates in the south-west corner of the square, the Canterbury Gates which lead to Canterbury Quad, are a reminder of these events.

Oriel College

Oriel College

The official name is 'The House of Blessed Mary the Virgin in Oxford' but the college got its present name from 'La Oriole' a house which stood on the site of the present front quad. Those who have studied at Oriel include Sir Walter Raleigh and Cecil Rhodes and amongst the Fellows is Henry Beeke the man who suggested the introduction of income tax to prime minister Pitt. Oriel in 1984 became the last of the men's colleges to admit women.

Corpus Christi College

Founded in 1517 by Bishop Foxe of Winchester, the man who baptised Henry VIII, this is one of the smallest Oxford colleges. Foxe was blind and after the college had been built he was guided round the front quad three times to trick him into thinking it was much bigger than it actually is. Corpus was the only college to save its silver plate from being melted down in the royalist cause during the Civil War. A former student, General Oglethorpe, founded the American state of Georgia.

Sundial - Corpus Christi College

Merton College *(see also walk 2 page 21)*

Founded in 1264 by Walter de Merton it is one of three colleges claiming to be the oldest in Oxford (the others are Balliol and University) and bases its claim on the fact that it was the first to have statutes. Merton has the oldest buildings in the entire university and has the oldest surviving medieval library. The collegiate layout set by Merton of staircases leading off quads was followed by every pre-19th century Oxford college. Mob Quad is the oldest quad in the oldest university in Britain.

Merton College

Beam Hall

One of the few remaining Oxford buildings which at one time was a medieval Hall. Its name is derived from a former owner Gilbert de Biham, who was also Chancellor of the University. In 1262 it passed from de Biham to St Frideswide's Priory and subsequently had many owners and uses.

The Queen's College *(see also walk 5 page 46)*

Founded in 1340 by Robert de Eglesfield, chaplain to Queen Philippa, who agreed that she and her successors should be patroness of the college. None of the original buildings survive as the college was completely rebuilt in the 17th and 18th centuries but the result is perhaps the finest example of classical architecture in Oxford. Each Christmas the Boar's Head dinner commemorates the feat of the medieval scholar who, being attacked by a wild boar in a nearby forest, thrust his copy of Aristotle down the unfortunate creature's throat, killed it, brought it back in triumph and feasted on it.

Wisdom, Eagle and Globe - The Queen's College Library

University College

Referred to as 'Univ' this is one of three colleges claiming to be the oldest in Oxford (the others are Balliol and Merton). In 1249 William of Durham bequeathed 310 marks to the university to buy property and to use the rents from that property to fund 12 Masters of Arts. Thus Univ had the first benefaction and its claim to be the oldest collegiate establishment is based on this. Former students include Bob Hawke and Bill Clinton.

All Souls College Tower

All Souls College *(see also walk 1 page 13)*

Legend has it that when the college was being built a mallard flew out of a drain and to commemorate this occurrence a strange ceremony takes place once every 100 years. On 14th January in the first year of each new century the Fellows, carrying lighted torches and sticks, go in procession to look for the missing duck!

St Mary the Virgin

(see also walk 1 page 13)

Notice the south porch entrance with its 'barley sugar' 17th century columns. The statue of the Virgin and Child was defaced during the Civil War when a passing soldier in Cromwell's army fired a volley at it but it was repaired in 1662. It was in this church that Archbishop Cranmer was tried for heresy in 1555, where John Wesley the founder of Methodism preached his famous 1774 sermon, and where John Keeble in 1833 delivered his Assize sermon which was the catalyst for the Oxford Movement.

Brasenose College

(see also walk 1 page 13)

Usually referred to as BNC the college was founded in 1509 and one of its first Principals, Alexander Nowell, is credited with the invention of bottled beer. Lawrence Washington, a former student and great-grandfather of the first American President, left behind a 1649 bill for 17s 6d which was finally paid by a visiting American lawyer in 1924.

St Mary the Virgin Porch

28

29　　*Schools Quad Main Entrance (Walk One)*

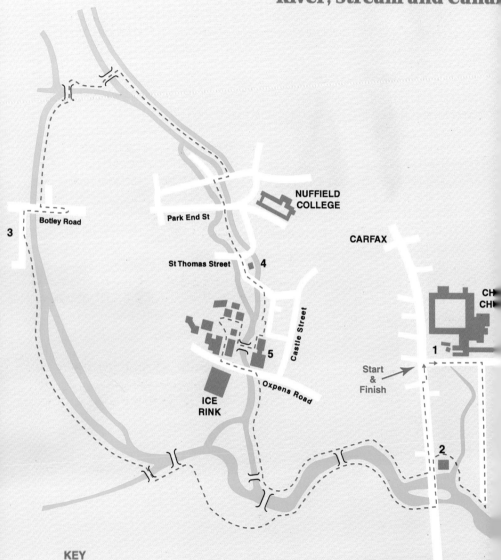

NUFFIELD COLLEGE

Botley Road

3

Park End St

St Thomas Street

4

CARFAX

CH
CH

Castle Street

1

5

Start
&
Finish

Oxpens Road

ICE
RINK

2

KEY

1 War Memorial Garden
2 Head of the River Public House
3 Osney Town
4 Castle Tower
5 Oxford College of Further Education

- - - - - - - - - - Route of the walk

Walk 4
RIVER, STREAM AND CANAL

Introduction
The first half mile of this walk is also part of walk 2 but it is such a pleasant half mile that it would be churlish to banish it simply to avoid repetition. The directions of this section are repeated to simplify route finding.

The walk itself is largely along towpaths although small sections pass through busy parts of the city. This variety however, adds to the sense of discovery of Oxford as an urban, rural and riverside city. There are many delightful spots along the way for picnicking and if you would like a restful stroll with changing views perhaps this is the one to try. Unfortunately, because of a few steps and gates, although the walk is flat, it is unsuitable for wheelchairs.

Length
The walk is 3 miles long over flat and easy ground and should take about an hour and a half to complete. Any time spent picnicking or relaxing should, of course, be added to this estimate.

Buildings
To ensure directions are clear and straightforward minimal information is included in the walk description on the buildings seen. However, the 'Additional Information' section on *pages 35-36* provides a brief overview of each of the locations printed in **bold type**.

Starting Point
The starting and finishing points of this circular walk are at the Memorial Garden gates in St Aldates, approximately 300 yards south of Carfax.

The Walk

Walk through the wrought iron gates into the **War Memorial Garden**. Notice the sword inlaid into the paving at the entrance with an inscription from John Bunyan's *Pilgrims Progress* 'My sword I give to him that shall succeed me in my pilgrimage'.

Christ Church Hall

Walk 5 or 6 paces into the Garden and pause to look at some of the buildings. On the left is **Christ Church** with **Tom Tower** and the Hall in full view, on the right is the north wing of the Faculty of Music containing the Bate Collection of English and European woodwind, brass and percussion instruments. Behind, across the road, is Alice's Shop where Alice of *Alice in Wonderland* and *Alice through the Looking Glass* bought her sweets. Alice in real life was Alice Liddell the daughter of the Dean of Christ Church.

Walk through the Garden, up two sets of three steps each, into **Christ Church Meadow**.

After a few yards, opposite the visitors entrance to Christ Church, turn right along Poplar Walk which was planted in 1872 by Alice's father Dean Liddell. Continue between the trees, along this very pleasant stretch of meadow which often has contented cattle grazing on your left, and after a quarter of a mile reach the River Thames or Isis as it is known hereabouts.

Head of the River pub

Turn right along the towpath which leads through a small spinney to a gate on the left. Go through the gate, over the bridge and follow the path to emerge on the busy Abingdon Road.

Turn left keeping **The Head of the River** pub on your left, cross the bridge and 30 yards after the bridge carefully cross the road to walk along the Thames Path, signposted to Osney, which will be reached after a further mile of delightful walking.

After a short while take the right fork, Jubilee Terrace, keeping the river immediately on your right and walk under the bridge ahead.

Just before the second bridge fork left and then keep to the right to walk through Grandpont Nature Park which swings in an arc before rejoining the towpath just before a railway bridge. Walk under the bridge keeping on the path which swings to the right across the Bulstake Stream, and pause at the memorial to Edgar George Wilson who lost his life in 1889 after rescuing two boys from drowning,

Continue through Osney Lock, built by prisoners of Oxford Gaol and opened in 1790, and soon skirt the terraced houses of **Osney Town**. Go up the steps on the left and across the bridge to reach Botley Road.

Turn right, and for safety's sake walk to the traffic lights before crossing the road. Once safely over Botley Road turn left towards the bridge crossing Abbey Road. Immediately before the bridge turn right to walk down to the towpath with the river now on the left.

Osney Lock

Occasionally this stretch of the towpath is flooded and the right turn is blocked
If this is the case walk up Abbey Road, to the end, then turn left
to rejoin the walk at the bridge referred to in the next paragraph.

After 300 yards cross a bridge and turn right along a pathway signposted to Oxford Canal. After a few yards walk under a series of railway bridges making sure to bend low to avoid banging your head. Cross the road keeping the stream on your right, over a footbridge, then turn immediately right over yet another bridge to Isis Lock.

Walk along the towpath with the **canal** and its moored longboats on the left, **Isis Lock** on the right, and very soon the steeple of **Nuffield College** clearly visible ahead.

When you emerge at Hythe Bridge Street turn right, walk for 20 yards and at the pavement end turn left to cross the road carefully before descending 10 steps and walking through a small park area. After a few yards walk up 7 steps, cross the road and walk down another set of 7 steps on the clearly signposted Mill Stream walk.

Moored Longboats

Castle Tower

Cross St Thomas Street and, keeping the **Castle Tower** on your left, walk down Paradise Street and over the bridge as far as the Mill Stream signpost just before Paradise Square. Turn right here, and veering left with the stream on your right, continue until the pathway emerges by a building and a car park. Here ignore the signpost and turn right to walk round the outside of the Oxford College of Further Education and over the footbridge. Turn right immediately after the footbridge to six steps. Turn left immediately after descending the steps and walk between the college buildings before taking the first turning on the left which leads past the road barriers to the main road with the Ice Rink directly ahead.

Cross the road at the traffic lights and turn left crossing the bridge over the Mill Stream. Immediately after the bridge turn right along a walkway with the stream on the right and houses on the left. After a quarter of a mile or so ignore a bridge on the right and pass under the archway of another bridge.

Continue along the path with the river on the right walking under yet another footbridge and soon a wrought iron gate across the pathway is reached. This gate does not signify that the way ahead is private so walk through the gate, and the next one, to reach Folly Bridge, a major traffic bearing bridge.

Turn left just before the heavy, wrought iron gates in front of the bridge and walk up to the main road. Turn left, cross the traffic lights ahead and walk to the next set of traffic lights where turn right to cross the road, then left to walk the 30 yards to the Memorial Gates and the finish of the walk.

Folly Bridge

Additional Information

War Memorial Garden
Laid out in 1925 the garden commemorates all Oxford men, whether from the city or the university, who died in the First World War.

Christ Church *(see also walk 3 page 19)*
Founded as Cardinal College in 1525 by Cardinal Wolsey but unfinished when he fell from power, the college was refounded as Christ Church in 1545 by Henry VIII. Perhaps the grandest of Oxford colleges it numbers amongst its alumnae 14 Prime Ministers, John Wesley the founder of Methodism, and William Penn the founder of Pennsylvania. The college chapel is also the cathedral of the Oxford diocese.

Tom Tower
Designed by Christopher Wren and built in 1682 above Wolsey's 1527 archway and turrets. Inside the tower is Great Tom, the loudest bell in Oxford, which chimes 101 times every evening at 9.05pm to recall the 101 students resident in 1682 and their curfew time of 9pm. However, as Great Tom keeps local time not GMT and since the college is 5 minutes west of Greenwich, the bell chimes at 9.05pm!

Christ Church Meadow
Part of the meadow was a gift from Lady Montacute who in 1454 was buried in the priory of St Frideswide: the priory was subsequently incorporated into the college chapel during the building of Christ Church. It is difficult to believe that during the 1950s and 1960s various schemes were put forward to build a road through the meadow and only intense opposition resulted in the plans finally being shelved in 1966.

The Head of the River
First mentioned as a Thames-side wharf in 1628 it became Wharf House in 1827 and a pub exactly 150 years later in 1977. It is named after the college bumping races held during the summer term.

Preparing for a Bump Race start

Osney Town

Although there has been an 'Osney' of various spellings hereabouts since 1200 the present suburb was built in the early 1850's. With a little imagination the layout resembles a compass and the streets, aptly named north, south, east and west, reinforce this picture.

Pond created from canal remnant - Nuffield College

Canal/Isis Lock *(see also walk 6 page 55)*

The canal took 22 years to build and when completed in 1791 had 42 locks, was crossed by 250 bridges and had cost £307,000. Isis Lock, built in 1796 to link the canal and the Thames, joins Osney Lock as another example on this walk of a lock built by Oxford Gaol prisoners.

Nuffield College *(see also walk 6 page 54)*

When Lord Nuffield bought the canal wharf he offered to build a college on part of the land to improve the visual approach to the west side of Oxford. His original intention was a college of Engineering and Accountancy but he was persuaded to change his mind and the college, which majors in social studies, aims to provide a link between industry and academia.

Castle Tower *(see also walk 6 Oxford Castle, page 55)*

St George's Tower was the first building in the castle and is one of the few surviving military buildings in England dating from the Norman Conquest. It is four storeys high, narrower at the top than at the base, and the walls are nine feet thick at ground level.

A view from the towpath

Radcliffe Camera and All Souls from inside The Queen's College

Walk 5

Outside the Medieval City

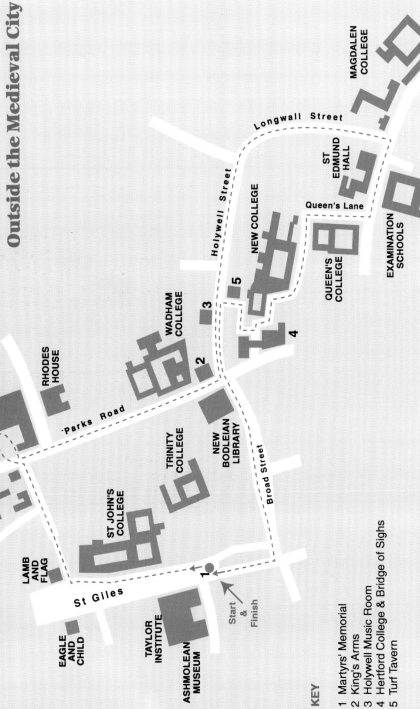

KEY

1 Martyrs' Memorial
2 King's Arms
3 Holywell Music Room
4 Hertford College & Bridge of Sighs
5 Turf Tavern

Route of the walk

Walk 5
OUTSIDE THE MEDIEVAL CITY

Introduction

In the early days Oxford was a small city with the rivers Thames and Cherwell providing natural defences on the south, west and east of the city. The first artificial defences date from Alfred the Great (853-901) and although the construction date of Oxford's first wall is unknown it was certainly in existence by 919 and was probably built 8 years earlier. Numerous improvements and extensions were undertaken over the centuries and the wall was virtually rebuilt 1226-40 *(see also walk 2 page 21)*.

This walk, although fully within the modern city is almost entirely outside of the old city boundaries. Many of the buildings seen are associated with major historical events including the Black Death, the religious upheavals of the 16th century and the Civil War: others, including 17th century pubs and a concert hall, reflect the social evolution of the city.

Length

This walk of a mile and a half passes many interesting and important buildings as well as wandering along leafy roads, medieval lanes and narrow alleyways. To get the best from this walk it should not be rushed and perhaps an hour or so should be allowed to complete it.

Buildings

To ensure directions are clear and straightforward minimal information is included in the walk description on the buildings seen. However, the 'Additional Information' section on *pages 43-47* provides a brief overview of each of the locations printed in **bold type**.

Starting Point

This circular walk starts and finishes at the Martyrs Memorial in St Giles.

The Walk

Standing at the **Martyrs Memorial** the Randolph Hotel is on your immediate left. Across Beaumont Street is the **Taylor Institute** with its prominent Ionic pillars and, just behind, the **Ashmolean Museum**.

Lamb and Flag Pub

Carefully cross the road and walk up the right hand pavement of St Giles, opposite the Taylor Institute, and after 100 yards reach the entrance tower of **St John's College** with its statue of St Bernard dating from, and a reminder of, the original Cistercian foundation. Continue for a further 150 yards to reach the 17th century **Lamb and Flag** pub. Directly opposite is the **Eagle and Child** favoured by the 17th century diarist Anthony Wood as well as by the 20th century Inklings.

Turn right down Lamb and Flag Passage, signposted to the University Museum, keeping the pub on your left hand side.

Walk under the magnificent horse chestnut tree and then through two sets of bollards to reach the main road ahead. The **University Museum** fronted by a large lawn is across the road slightly to the left. Cross the road to the museum and notice carvings have been completed around only one of the windows. The carvings on this 'cat window', second on the right from the entrance tower, were originally of monkeys but opposition to the theory of evolution forced a change.

Turn round for a wonderful view through the trees of **Keble College** with its polychromatic brickwork arousing strong feelings amongst supporters and opponents alike. It is said that John Ruskin, the founder of the *Ruskin School of Drawing and Fine Art*, would take a 30 minute detour to avoid catching sight of the building.

Walk back to the road and turn left. After a few yards cross over South Parks Road making sure to look left to see the domed roof of **Rhodes House**. Continue for 200 yards arriving opposite the blue wrought iron gates of **Trinity College** which give superb views of the perfectly manicured lawns. A few yards further, on the left, is Christopher Wren's alma mater **Wadham College**. Dorothy Wadham instructed that only men were to be employed by the college, with the single exception of the laundress - and she had to be *'of such age, condition, and reputation as to be above suspicion'*. A little further brings us to the **King's Arms** on the left, and opposite the stark **New Bodleian Library** formally opened by King George VI in an embarrassing 1940 ceremony when the silver key broke in the lock.

City Wall seen through New College entrance

Turn left at the traffic lights and walk down Holywell Street passing on the left **Holywell Music Room** probably the oldest still functioning concert hall in the world. Continue along this street of charming, mainly 16th and 17th century houses, beyond Mansfield Road, to **New College** entrance on the right. Look through to see part of the substantial and well preserved section of the old city wall which is in the college grounds.

A little further on swing right with the road into Longwall Street, named after the city wall and not the 1467 **Magdalen College** wall on the left. Soon after entering Longwall Street, on the right, is the original Longwall Garage where in 1912 William Morris built his first car, the prototype of the bull-nosed Morris Oxford. Take a moment, a few yards further on, to look through the gate on the right where behind the trees is another section of the old city wall complete with a bastion.

Continue to the traffic lights and pause on the corner to look left to Magdalen College tower. From the top of this tower the college choir sings at 6 am every May Day morning whilst several thousand people make merry in the street below.

Award of an MA Degree

Turn right along High Street with the tower of St Mary the Virgin clearly visible on the bend in the road ahead. Across on the left after the Eastgate Hotel are the **Examination Schools** with two sculptured panels over the main entrance showing a viva voce examination and the award, by touching the successful candidate's forehead with a bible, of an MA degree.

Turn right into the first opening on the right, Queen's Lane, keeping **The Queen's College** on your left. After 30 yards on the right is **St Edmund Hall** the only survivor of the medieval Halls which preceded colleges and in which students were provided with accommodation and tuition. The college library, formerly the church of **St Peter-in-the-East** is directly ahead. Continue along Queen's Lane described by John Betjeman as *'a little lane like Oxford used to be before the petrol age'* with the towers of All Souls College and the dome of the Radcliffe Camera *(see walk 1)* clearly visible. Look up to your right to see the gargoyles on the southern wall of New College.

New College Tower

As the road turns right and then quickly left look behind to see the entrance tower of New College whose Holywell Street entrance, with a view of the old city wall, was past earlier on this walk. Continue along the twists and turns of the lane and notice on the right about 30 yards before the **Bridge of Sighs** the house, with an observatory on the roof, where Edmund Halley of comet fame lived. He was an undergraduate at Queen's College and later, 1703-43, Savilian Professor of Geometry.

Just before reaching the Bridge of Sighs which from this direction wonderfully frames the Sheldonian Theatre *(see walk 1)* turn right down a narrow alleyway, St Helen's Passage, which leads to the 17th century **Turf Tavern** where reputedly the last cockfight in England took place.

Turn left in front of the pub with a section of the old city wall on the right and a very good view of New College tower ahead, and pass a small hotel and some guest houses seemingly huddled for safety outside of but close to the city wall, and emerge into Holywell Street opposite the Holywell Music Room seen earlier on the walk.

Turn left and cross the road at the traffic lights to walk along the right hand pavement of Broad Street past Blackwell's book shop. The main buildings on both sides of this section of the walk - the Clarendon, the Sheldonian Theatre and the Museum of the History of Science on the left, and Trinity and Balliol Colleges on the right - are described in *walk 1.*

Balliol College

Forty yards beyond the entrance to Balliol College notice both the plaque on the wall referring to the execution of the three martyrs and the cross in the centre of the road marking the approximate spot where they perished.

Continue along Broad Street crossing the small road coming from the right to reach the main road where a right turn is made before reaching after another 150 yards the Martyrs Memorial and the end of the walk.

Additional Information

Martyrs' Memorial
Commemorates three martyrs who were burned at the stake in Oxford during the reign of Queen Mary, a Catholic. Bishops Latimer and Ridley were martyred in 1555 and Archbishop Cranmer in 1556. In the 19th century a public appeal was launched resulting in this memorial, designed by Sir George Gilbert Scott, being built in 1843. Cranmer holding his bible faces north, Latimer with head bowed and arms crossed faces west, and Ridley east.

Taylor Institute
Known as 'the Taylorian' and completed in 1844 the building houses lecture theatres, offices and the main libraries of the Modern Languages Faculty. The female statues on top of the four Ionic columns represent France, Italy, Germany and Spain whose languages are the main ones taught in the building.

Ashmolean Museum
In the early 17th century John Tradescant's collection of rarities in south London was opened to the public for a charge of 6d. Known as *Tradescant's Ark* it was considered to be the best museum of its kind in the world. The collection was increased by John's son and in 1656 most of the specimens were listed in the *Musaeum Tradescantium*, the first museum catalogue to be printed in Britain. Elias Ashmole inherited the collection and bequeathed it, together with his own collection, to the university. This became the Ashmolean Museum which opened in 1683 in what is now the Museum of the History of Science in Broad Street. In 1894 the natural history items were transferred to the **University Museum** and the rest of the collection to the present building.

St John's College
Founded by a merchant tailor Sir Thomas White in 1555, the year Latimer and Ridley were martyred, and named after St John the Baptist, the patron saint of tailors. The college was originally St Bernard's, founded in 1437 as a college for Cistercian students but dissolved in 1539 and subsequently bought by Sir Thomas White. One of its first Fellows, Edmund Campion was hung, drawn and quartered when the religious tide turned yet again under Elizabeth I.

St John's College

Lamb and Flag

Named after the crest of the owners **St John's College** who opened it as a tavern in 1695. The Monday lunchtime meetings of the Inklings (see **Eagle and Child** below) continued here until Lewis's death in November 1963.

Eagle and Child

Named after the Earl of Derby whose family crest is a coronet with eagle and child and known locally as 'the bird and the baby' it has been on this site since 1650. From the mid 1930's until 1962 it was the regular weekly lunchtime meeting place of C S Lewis, J R R Tolkien and their circle of literary friends known as The Inklings. In 1962 they transferred their allegiance across the road to the **Lamb and Flag.**

University Museum

University Museum

Completed in 1858 this museum of natural history contains a wonderful exhibition of dinosaur and other skeletons, the remains of a Dodo, plus vast zoology, mineralogy and geology displays. The museum leads through to the Pitt Rivers museum housing one of the world's finest collections of anthropological and archaeological exhibits.

Keble College *(see also walk 7 page 62)*

Keble College Chapel

Founded in 1868 Keble is the first Oxford college to be built of brick, the first to be built by public subscription rather than a wealthy benefactor and the first to be built with corridors instead of rooms off staircases. Named after John Keble, a leader of the Oxford Movement which sought a return by the Anglican Church to the 'pure church' of the early Fathers, in its early years it especially catered for young men of humble background needing financial assistance who wished to become clergymen.

Rhodes House *(see also walk 7 page 62)*

Opened in 1929 as a memorial to Cecil Rhodes it is now used as offices for the Rhodes Trust. On the copper-domed roof is the Zimbabwe bird the national symbol of Zimbabwe, formerly Rhodesia. Eighty five Rhodes scholarships are awarded each year on the basis of academic and all round qualities to graduates from 18 countries. The first Rhodes scholars arrived in 1903 and former scholars include Bill Clinton, Norman Manley former prime minister of Jamaica, and the actor Kris Kristofferson.

Trinity College *(see also walks 1 and 7 pages 11 and 63)*
The wrought-iron gates, erected in 1713, do not open and are lifted off to allow marquees and furniture to be delivered for garden parties. At the far end of the garden is the three-sided Garden Quad the north side of which was designed by Christopher Wren. An interesting example of intercollegiate co-operation is demonstrated by Trinity allowing men from All Souls, a non-rowing college, to row in its college eight.

Wadham College *(see also walk 7 page 63)*
When Nicholas Wadham died in 1609 his will included the provision of a new college at Oxford. His formidable widow, Dorothy, controlling every aspect of the work from her home more than 100 miles away in Somerset, carried out his plan to such good effect that Wadham was founded in 1612 only three years after her husband's death. The original statutes prevented the Warden (Head) from marrying and it required a special Act of Parliament nearly 200 years later in 1806 to change this situation.

Wadham College

King's Arms *(see also walk 7 page 60)*
The king in question is James I who was reigning when the pub opened in 1607 as an inn. Although parts of the original inn remain most of what can be seen is 18th century. The upper floors have been converted into accommodation for Wadham College students.

New Bodleian Library *(see also walk 7 page 63)*
Designed by Sir Giles Scott the 11 floors, three of which are underground, are cleverly arranged in a pyramid-like shape to avoid overpowering nearby buildings. This building is part of a central group of Bodleian Library buildings linked underground and containing nearly seven million books and 100 miles of shelving.

Holywell Music Room *(see also walk 7 page 60)*
When opened in 1748 it was considered to be Europe's finest concert hall. Considerable alterations took place after 1793 and the room was used for a variety of purposes until reverting to purely musical use in 1901 when the lease was acquired by Oxford University Musical Union. It is now jointly administered by Wadham College and the Faculty of Music.

Holywell Music Room

New College

New College *(see also walk 7 page 61)*
New College, founded in 1379, was the seventh Oxford college but the first to admit undergraduates: until then undergraduates lived in Academic Halls and colleges admitted only graduates. The college's founder, William of Wykeham Bishop of Winchester, also founded Winchester School to ensure a supply of students properly grounded in Latin grammar and for nearly 500 years, until 1857, only members of Wykeham's family and boys from Winchester School were admitted to New College. The full name of the college is St. Mary College of Winchester in Oxford but it was called New College to differentiate it from another St. Mary's now called Oriel!

Magdalen College *(see also walk 2 page 20)*
By 1458 the 13th century hospital of St John the Baptist had been reduced to having only five patients. The site and buildings were transferred and became incorporated into the newly founded Magdalen College. However the college buildings seen from Longwall Street are the much more recent 19th and 20th century additions.

Examination Schools

Examination Schools
Until 1882 when examinations were first held here they took place in Schools Quad *(walk 1)*. In addition to holding examinations the building houses the university's portrait gallery, is frequently used for lectures and conferences, and during both world wars became a hospital.

The Queen's College *(see also walk 3 page 27)*
Jeremy Bentham, the future political philosopher, arrived at Queen's in 1760 at the tender age of 12 and his letters home provide a fascinating insight into 18th century undergraduate life. In one he writes of his daily routine explaining that his morning is taken up with prayers, lectures in logic, ablutions and then lunch at 12.30. The classics were taught in the evening, geography on Thursday afternoons and Saturday mornings were devoted to exercise.

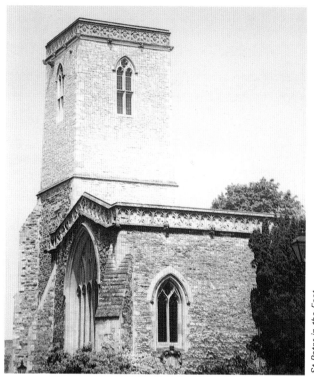

St Peter-in-the-East

St Edmund Hall

Named after St Edmund of Abingdon who in the 1190's taught in a house on this site when he was a Regent Master in the Arts. Known as Teddy Hall and founded in 1238 it gained full college status in 1957. A former student, Lord Methuen became ambassador to Portugal and in 1703 signed a treaty which introduced port, and probably gout, into England.

St Peter-in-the-East

The church, which replaced a 10th century timber church, was first recorded in 1086 and has been described as *'the first church of stone that appeared in these parts'*. It was converted to St Edmund Hall library in 1970.

Bridge of Sighs *(see also walk 1 page 12)*

Although the building of the bridge was strongly opposed by New College it has become a much admired architectural feature of the city.

Turf Tavern

Beginning life as a malthouse, it became a cider house in 1775, the *Spotted Cow* inn about 1790 and the *Turf Tavern* in 1847.

Walk 6
Old and New

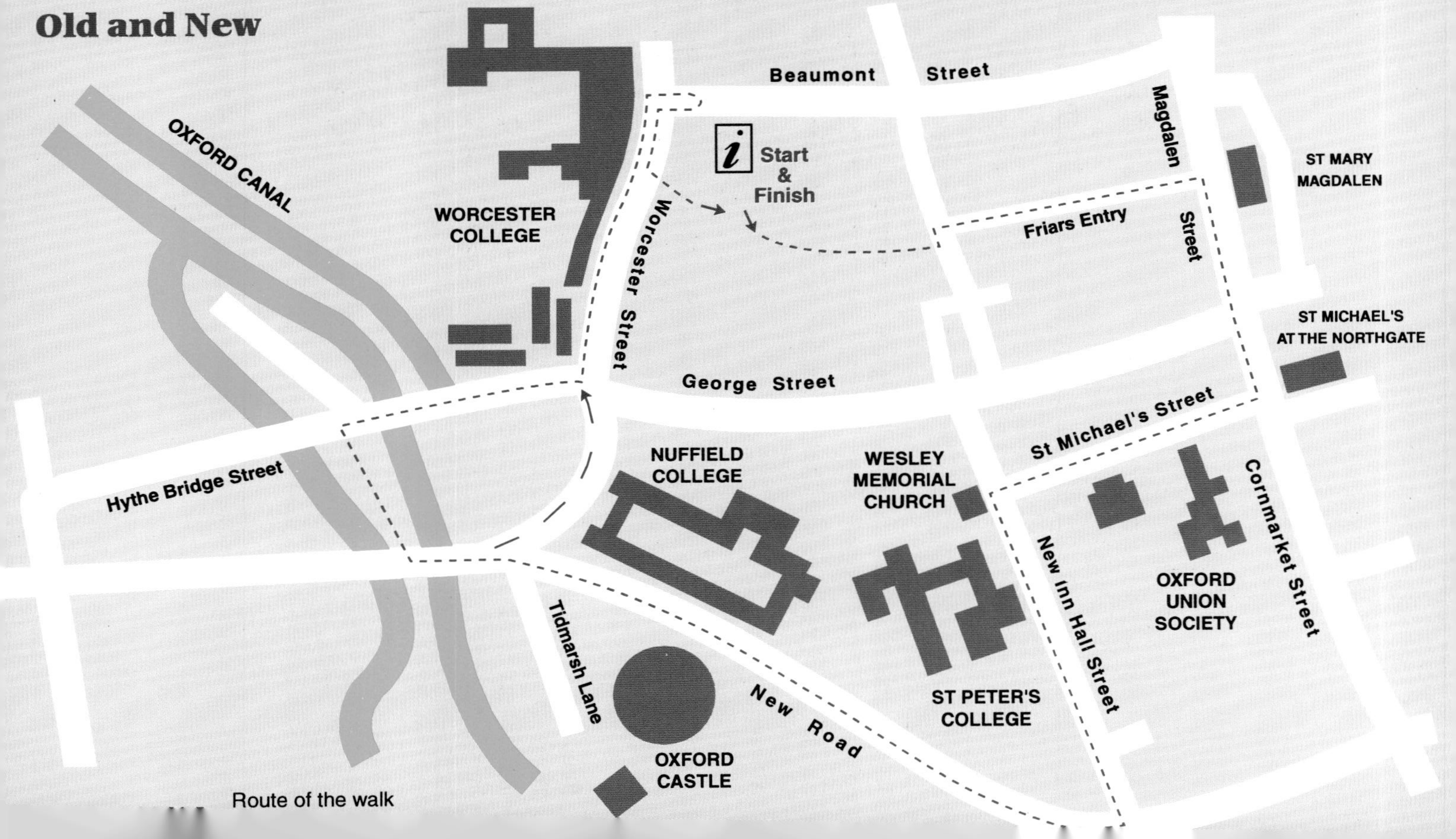

ST MARY MAGDALEN

ST MICHAEL'S AT THE NORTHGATE

Cornmarket Street

OXFORD UNION SOCIETY

Magdalen Street

Friars Entry

St Michael's Street

New Inn Hall Street

ST PETER'S COLLEGE

Beaumont Street

i Start & Finish

George Street

WESLEY MEMORIAL CHURCH

New Road

NUFFIELD COLLEGE

Worcester Street

OXFORD CASTLE

WORCESTER COLLEGE

Tidmarsh Lane

OXFORD CANAL

Hythe Bridge Street

Route of the walk

Walk 6
OLD AND NEW

Introduction

Politics, religion, commerce and academia are amongst the influences which have formed the modern Oxford and this walk touches on each of these strands. Although much of the walk is in the shopping area of the town the walk includes the two oldest buildings in Oxford, two of the newer colleges, the first church in Oxford to restore the Book of Common Prayer, the church at the centre of Methodist work amongst Oxford students, and the canal so influential from the late 18th to the early 20th centuries.

Length

This one mile walk takes in crowded shopping streets as well as quieter non-commercial areas. As there is much to see and investigate along the way you should allow perhaps three quarters of an hour to complete the walk.

Alternative Route To Avoid Steps

This walk is flat but towards the end there are two lots of steps and an alternative route is given for this small section for those wishing to avoid the steps. The alternative does not affect either the length of the walk or the time required to complete it.

Buildings

To ensure directions are clear and straightforward minimal information is included in the walk description on the buildings seen. However, the 'Additional Information' section on *pages 52-55* provides a brief overview of each of the locations printed in **bold type**.

Starting Point

This circular walk starts and finishes at the Tourist Information Centre in Gloucester Green.

The Walk

With your back to the Tourist Information Centre turn left and walk underneath the archway into Gloucester Square noting the plaque on the archway wall commemorating the opening of the square in 1989. Walk across the left hand side of the square and turn left at the end through the bollards.

St Mary Magdalen Church

Turn right almost immediately down the 17th century Friar's Entry passageway thought to be named after the Carmelite friars who lived near Gloucester Green and who would have used this route on their journeys to and from **St Mary Magdalen**'s church. Emerge opposite the church which, unusually, is wider (85 feet) than it is long (80 feet).

Turn right and after 50 yards cross George Street and continue to St Michael's Street. Opposite is the tower of **St Michael's at the Northgate**, the oldest building in Oxford and one of the very few surviving Saxon buildings in the country.

Turn right into St Michael's Street with the Wesley Memorial Methodist Church clearly visible ahead. Halfway down the street, on the left hand side, is the **Oxford Union Society** described by former Prime Minister Harold Macmillan as *'unique in that it has provided an unrivalled training ground for debates in the Parliamentary style which no other debating society in any democratic country can equal'.*

Wesley Memorial Church

Continue past Frewin Annexe, additional accommodation for Brasenose College students built on the site of the medieval Frewin Hall, to the end of the street.

Turn left into New Inn Hall Street leaving on your right the **Wesley Memorial Methodist Church** built in 1878 to celebrate the admission of Non-Conformists to the university. After 10 yards notice the plaque on the wall concerning St Edward's School and Mackworth Hall, yet another of the academic halls once thriving in this area.

50

Across the road is one of the newer Oxford colleges, **St Peter's**, founded in 1929 although the entrance is a 1797 former Oxford Company Canal building. After another 30 yards on the wall on the left hand side of the street, just beyond the gates on the right, is a plaque recording John Wesley's preaching in 1783 in the first Methodist meeting house in Oxford.

Continue to the end of the street and turn right into Bonn Square past the stone monument on the corner commemorating the opening of the square. Across on the left is the Westgate Shopping Centre built on the site of the old West Gate of the city.

Walk ahead down New Road keeping to the right hand pavement. Across the road is the castle-like County Hall which has been described as *'quite the most abominable pseudo-Gothic Assize Court in all England'*. Just beyond on the right look through the opening to St Peter's College car park at the large building which was once Canal House and is now St Peter's College Master's lodgings.

Ahead on the right is another of the newer colleges, **Nuffield College**, built in the style of a Cotswold manor house, specialising in the social sciences and aiming to provide a bridge between industry and academia. Directly opposite is the rather older 11th century **Oxford Castle** mound, now overgrown but once free from grass and deliberately kept as slippery as possible to make capture more difficult.

Continue and carefully cross over Worcester Street. Once safely on the other side look down Tidmarsh Lane for a perfect view of the castle tower.

Oxford Castle Mound

To avoid 2 sets of steps adjacent to the canal ignore the next paragraph, turn right and walk 50 yards up Worcester Street to rejoin the main walk at the traffic lights.

Continue for 50 yards before turning right down 7 steps to a small, peaceful park with the **canal** on the right. Walk through this pleasant, green area, up the 10 steps at the far end and turn right to walk to the traffic lights and rejoin the alternative route.

Turn left at the traffic lights *(straight on for those taking the alternative walk)* and cross the road with care. Continue to the next traffic lights with, on the left, the gated entrance to **Worcester College**, the only Oxford college with a lake in its gardens.

Location Pillar - Beaumont Palace

Turn right at the traffic lights to Beaumont Street and walk for just 10 yards to read the carved pillar commemorating the birth at **Beaumont Palace** in 1157 of Richard the Lionheart, probably the only English King to be born in Oxford (some say Richard's brother King John was also born here but this is not certain).

Cross to the other side of Beaumont Street and walk back down Worcester Street for 20 yards before turning left at the signpost for the Tourist Information Centre and the end of the walk.

Additional Information

St Mary Magdalen

Nothing remains of the Saxon church which once stood on this site and only the foundations of the subsequent Norman church have survived. The church was rebuilt in 1194, extended and restored in the late 13th century, and extended again by the Carmelite friars around 1320. Further work was undertaken in the 16th century and in 1841 a major restoration, including the complete rebuilding of the northern aisle, was completed with money left over from the building of the Martyrs Memorial *(see walk 5)*. The church, which in 1660 was the first in England to restore the Book of Common Prayer, is High Anglican.

St Michael's at the Northgate

Only the tower, probably built around 1050, remains of the original church. The present church is 13th century onwards and has been much altered over the years. The tower was connected to the North Gate, the strongest of the city gates which had a tower on either side, framing the gate and portcullis, with the Bocardo Prison above. The three martyrs were held in this prison before being burned at the stake in what is now Broad Street *(see walk 5)*.

Oxford Union Society

This is not the student's union but the debating forum founded in 1825 out of the two years old Oxford Union Debating Society. Former officers of the Union include five Prime Ministers as well as numerous cabinet ministers, politicians, lawyers and distinguished men and women from almost every walk of life. The library is the largest lending library in the University.

St Michael's at the Northgate

Wesley Memorial Methodist Church

Opened in 1878 the church is the centre for Methodist work among Oxford students through the John Wesley Society. New Inn Hall Street, which takes its name from the academic hall of the same name once situated in this street, is closely linked with Methodism as Samuel Wesley was a student at the Hall and his son John had his first preaching houses at numbers 32 and 34.

St Peter's College

Prior to becoming Bishop of Liverpool, Francis Chavasse had been rector of St Peter-le-Bailey in New Inn Hall Street. On his retirement he returned to live in his former rectory and founded St Peter's with the aim of providing an Oxford education for men who could not otherwise afford college life (in 1929 there was no co-education at Oxford). The Chavasse family was remarkable and during the First World War Francis's son Noel won the VC, bar and the MC, and his twin brothers Christopher and Bernard each won the MC. Christopher became the first Master of St Peter's and later Bishop of Rochester. The former church of St Peter-le-Bailey is now the college chapel.

Nuffield College Tower

Nuffield College

(see also walk 4 page 36)

Founded in 1937 by William Morris (Viscount Nuffield) who introduced car manufacturing to the city. The college was the first graduate only college apart from All Souls *(see walks 1 and 3)* and the first to admit both men and women. World War Two and its aftermath caused building work to be delayed and cut back resulting in the 160 foot tower, higher than Magdalen's *(see walks 2 and 5),* becoming a library rather than the chapel tower. In this way it became the first secular tower to be built in the city for two centuries.

Oxford Castle *(see also walk 4 Castle Tower, page 36)*
Built in 1071 for William the Conqueror by Robert d'Oilly to guard the crossing of the river Thames, this was one of a number of castles built one days march apart to enable travelling soldiers to sleep safely at night. The mound or 'motte' is 64 feet high, the diameter at road level is 210 feet and at the top 81 feet.

Canal *(see also walk 4 page 36)*
The canal, which connected Oxford with the Coventry canal, was completed in 1791, was 91 miles long and enabled better and cheaper coal to be brought to the city from the Midlands. Previously coal had been shipped to London and then brought up the Thames. However, after only four years Oxford was left without coal when, during the bitter winter of 1795, the canal froze over for 10 weeks. The city was finally relieved by horse drawn icebreakers.

Osney Lock

Worcester College
(see also walk 8 page 69)
Gloucester College, a Benedictine monastic college founded on this site in 1283, became derelict following the dissolution of the monasteries.
Twenty years later in 1560 the buildings were purchased and converted into Gloucester Hall, an academic hall operating under the guidance of St John's College. A chequered existence followed and by 1701 there were no undergraduates at all. Eventually the freehold was bought from St John's with money left in the will of a wealthy Worcestershire landowner, Sir Thomas Cookes, and in 1714 Worcester College was founded.

Beaumont Palace *(see also walk 8 page 69)*
Built by Henry I who first came here in 1133 this became a sizeable palace which included two chapels as well as the usual extensive living accommodation, stabling and storage required by a medieval monarch. However, within 150 years it was in decline: by the end of the 13th century it was no longer used as a royal residence, by the beginning of the 14th century its stone and timber had been removed to repair Oxford Castle, and finally in 1318 Edward II gave what was left of the buildings to the White Friars (Carmelites).

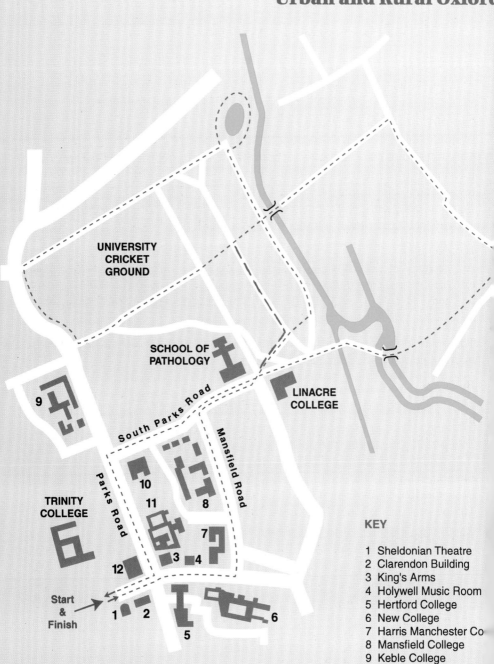

UNIVERSITY
CRICKET
GROUND

SCHOOL OF
PATHOLOGY

LINACRE
COLLEGE

9

South Parks Road

Mansfield Road

Parks Road

TRINITY
COLLEGE

10

11

8

7

12

3

4

Start
&
Finish

1

2

6

5

KEY

1 Sheldonian Theatre
2 Clarendon Building
3 King's Arms
4 Holywell Music Room
5 Hertford College
6 New College
7 Harris Manchester Co
8 Mansfield College
9 Keble College
10 Rhodes House
11 Wadham College
12 New Bodleian Library

- - - - - - - - - Route of the walk

— — — Shorter walk only

Walk 7
URBAN AND RURAL OXFORD

Introduction
There are pleasantly mixed views on this walk with the residential and university buildings of the first and last half miles contrasting agreeably with the park, countryside and water of the middle section.

Almost a mile and a half of the walk is in the University Parks. Always referred to as 'the Parks' this area of nearly 100 acres belonging to the University is widely used by the local population for walking, playing and watching sport, family outings and general relaxation. Referred to in the Domesday Book (1086) as *'thirty acres of meadow near the wall and a mill'* it became, 600 years later, an artillery base for the royalist forces during the Civil War (1642-46).

Length
As the route of this walk is roughly in a figure of 8 the easterly loop can be excluded restricting the walk to two and a half miles. The inclusion of the loop will add a mile. Depending on the option chosen you should allow either an hour and a half or two hours to complete the walk.

The walking is flat and easy although after heavy rain half a mile of the optional loop can be a little muddy underfoot.

Buildings
To ensure directions are clear and straightforward minimal information is included in the walk description on the buildings seen. However, the 'Additional Information' section on *pages 60-63* provides a brief overview of each of the locations printed in **bold type**.

Starting Point
Both the longer and shorter walks start and finish opposite the Sheldonian Theatre, less than half a mile from Carfax.

Restrictions
To prevent the acquisition of a public right of way the Parks are closed each year on the Monday of St Giles Fair and it is not possible to complete the walk on that day. As the Monday in question is in early September the probability is the closure will not conflict with your plans, but just in case, and also to give you an unusual question for a party quiz, the method of calculating the closure day is *the Monday following the first Sunday after St Giles' day (1st September)*

The Parks also close at dusk each day.

The Walk

Blackwell's

Start opposite the **Sheldonian Theatre** on the Blackwell's side of Broad Street and with Blackwell's on your left walk towards the traffic lights, crossing them to reach Holywell Street. Keeping the **King's Arms** on your left walk straight ahead past the **Holywell Music Room** to Mansfield Road the first street on the left. From here the entire frontage of **New College**, across the road, can be seen in a single glance.

Turn left up Mansfield Road which contains two of Oxford's newest colleges, both of which received their Royal Charters as full colleges in the mid 1990's. The first, **Harris Manchester**, with its imposing Gothic Revival main buildings. is reached after 50 yards. Opposite is the School of Geography. Continue ahead, crossing Savile Road, to reach **Mansfield College** one of the smallest as well as one of the newest of Oxford's full colleges. Directly opposite the college is the Institute of Virology and Environmental Microbiology, part of the Natural Environment Research Council.

Continue to the top of the road, turn right and walk 25 yards to the traffic lights before crossing to the far side of South Parks Road. Continue past the Department of Plant Sciences and the **School of Pathology**, the red bricked building on the left, where Professor Howard Florey carried out his pioneering work with penicillin.

Immediately after the private car park, and before reaching **Linacre College** the brick building directly ahead, turn left through wooden gates into the University Parks passing South Lodge on your right. Follow the path to the right keeping the mini-roundabout with its three silver birch trees on your left and go through the bollards to take the middle of three paths directly ahead.

Lily Pond

After 100 yards ignore two paths joining from the left but, after a further 40 yards, turn left with the track keeping the river Cherwell on your right. Continue alongside this stretch of the river which is very popular for punting, and pass a bridge to reach a large lily pond, built in 1925 and now home to several varieties of waterfowl.

58

Keeping the pond on your left walk around it until the path swings right, away from the pond, near a seat dedicated to the memory of John St L Philpot. Keep to the path and continue straight ahead ignoring all other paths joining from both left and right but noticing, after a short while, the **university cricket ground** on the left.

After a third of a mile, 20 yards before the gate leading out of the Parks, turn left with the path which swings in a wide arc with the uninspiring, functional buildings of the Science Triangle visible across the road.

At the next path junction, with the chapel of **Keble College** clearly visible diagonally right, turn left and after 20 yards keep to the left fork and walk straight ahead for a quarter of a mile.

If you do not wish to walk the optional mile follow the directions
in the next paragraph and then turn to page 60.

After passing the back of the cricket pavilion a crossing of the paths is reached 50 yards before a bridge spanning the river. Turn right to pass, on the right, a seat dedicated to the memory of Peter Hancock and continue for 300 yards before taking the right fork which leads directly to the gate used to enter the Parks. Walk through the gate and turn right along South Parks Road.

If you wish to complete the full
walk ignore the previous paragraph

After passing the back of the cricket pavilion carry on for 100 yards to reach a bridge spanning the Cherwell. Walk over the bridge and continue along the footpath for 400 yards until a T-junction is reached. Turn right at the junction passing, on the left, first the sports grounds of St Catherine's and Exeter colleges and then Park Farm. Soon after the farm turn right immediately in front of a housing estate, walk over a cattle grid and then straight ahead along the track for 400 yards before recrossing the Cherwell.

Footbridge to exit Parks

After crossing the river ignore the gate on the left and continue along the path to cross a further bridge with playing fields on the left. After a few yards take the right hand fork clearly marked 'Pedestrians Only' and after 200 yards reach South Parks Road and continue ahead.

On the left is the stark 1960's concrete building of the Department of Zoology and Psychology designed by Sir Leslie Martin. Walk for 100 yards to the traffic lights, cross the road and continue ahead passing the functional buildings of the science area which lie across the road.

Zimbabwe Bird - Rhodes House

Pass **Rhodes House** on the left and the Inorganic Chemistry building on the right to reach the end of South Parks Road then turn left into Parks Road. After 200 yards reach the much photographed blue wrought iron gates and garden quad of **Trinity College** and a little further on the left, **Wadham College**, used in the filming of *'Brideshead Revisited'*. Walk past the **New Bodleian Library** on the right to the traffic lights to cross the road and reach the end of the walk.

Additional Information

Sheldonian Theatre *(see also walk 1 page 11)*
Until the Sheldonian was completed in 1669 major university ceremonies took place in the church of St Mary the Virgin *(see walks 1 and 3)*. Today students come here at least twice during the course of their time at Oxford; first at the beginning of their studies for matriculation, the ceremony at which they become members of the university, and then at the end for their degree ceremony.

King's Arms Pub

King's Arms *(see also walk 5 page 45)*
The original buildings on this site were erected by Augustinian friars in 1268. Nowadays the pub is very popular with both dons and students and is said to have more brains per square inch than anywhere else in Oxford. However as this view is normally voiced after the consumption of large quantities of alcohol its accuracy is perhaps open to doubt.

Holywell Music Room *(see also walk 5 page 45)*
Built to provide a permanent home for the performance of concerts previously given in college halls, it has a seating capacity of 250 people and is thought to be the oldest, still functioning, music room in the world.

60

New College

(see also walk 5 page 46)
New College had an extraordinary privilege which enabled its members to obtain university degrees without the chore of taking university examinations. In 1800 when the university introduced written examinations to supersede 'vivas' New College students were barred from sitting them and took college examinations instead. However, to ensure high standards the college examinations were more difficult and eventually the students rebelled resulting in the privilege being voluntarily renounced in 1843.

New College Tower

Harris Manchester College

From 1581 until 1871 religious tests prevented those who did not subscribe to the Thirty-Nine Articles of the Anglican Church from studying at Oxford. Manchester College, founded in Manchester in 1786 on the principle of religious liberty, provided higher education for those debarred from Oxford on religious grounds. The college which changed location 3 times before settling in Oxford in 1889, became a full college of the university in 1996. The college admits only mature students.

Mansfield College

Although the abolition of religious tests in 1871 enabled non-Anglicans to study at Oxford, it was soon felt that the Free Churches would benefit from *'a more vigorous, organised yet academic'* environment. As a result, in 1886, the Congregational Churches closed Spring Hill College, their theological college in Birmingham, and moved to Oxford. The name was changed as a tribute to the Mansfield family who had founded the Birmingham college in 1838. Since 1985 there has been a period of expansion and change and in 1995 Mansfield became a full college of the university.

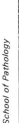
School of Pathology

Although pathology was first taught at Oxford as part of general medicine, by 1845 it had become a separate subject. The present building was formally opened in 1927 and it was here that Florey, an Oxford shoemaker's son born in Adelaide, Australia, together with Boris Chain, built on Alexander Fleming's discovery of penicillin and turned it into a life saving drug.

Linacre College

A graduate college established in 1962 to provide a collegiate base for graduate students and granted its charter as a fully self-governing college in 1986. The college is named after Thomas Linacre (1460-1524) who numbered Thomas Moore, Erasmus and Wolsey amongst his pupils.

University Cricket Ground

Opened in 1881 the ground is one of the few in the country where first class cricket can be watched free of charge. The pavilion, designed by T G Jackson, was built in 1880.

Keble College

Keble College *(see also walk 5 page 44)*

The chapel, which was paid for by William Gibbs who had made his fortune selling guano, was opened in 1876. It was never consecrated because this would have involved the participation of the Bishop of Oxford who was deeply mistrusted by the college Council.

Rhodes House *(see also walk 5 page 44)*

Rhodes scholarships, which are normally held for two years, are open to both men and women between the ages of 19 and 25. Nearly 100 selection committees throughout the world select scholars on the basis of academic record, confidential testimonials and personal interview.

Trinity College

(see walks 1 and 5 pages 11 and 45)
Trinity is set back on all sides, including its Broad Street frontage, and although close to the centre of the city is the most secluded of the old colleges. Terence Rattigan, the playwright, was a student here but never graduated saying he didn't want to be 'marked out for life by getting a degree.' The explorer Richard Burton on the other hand was rusticated (temporarily expelled) and confident that his family didn't know the meaning of the word explained he had been given an extra holiday because he had taken a double first.

Trinity College

Wadham College *(see walk 5 page 45)*

'Breakfast Meetings' conjure up visions of high powered executives solving major problems early in the morning, but a breakfasting club founded in 1842 had altogether different objectives. The decisions of the Wadham Beefsteak Club whose aim was to foster *'good fellowship by periodical meetings at breakfast'* majored on food. Initially only beefsteak and sausages could be served, but after much discussion and deep thought it was decided, three years later, that if sausages were out of season kidneys could be substituted. Mutton chops, however, never received the seal of approval.

New Bodleian Library *(see walk 5 page 45)*

In 1610 Thomas Bodley who refounded the university library which now bears his name, came to an agreement with the Stationers Office giving the Bodleian the right to a free copy of every book registered at Stationers Hall. As a result each week a large lorry delivers a free copy of every book published in this country during the previous week. There are four other 'copyright' libraries: the British Library, the national libraries of Scotland and Wales, and Cambridge University Library.

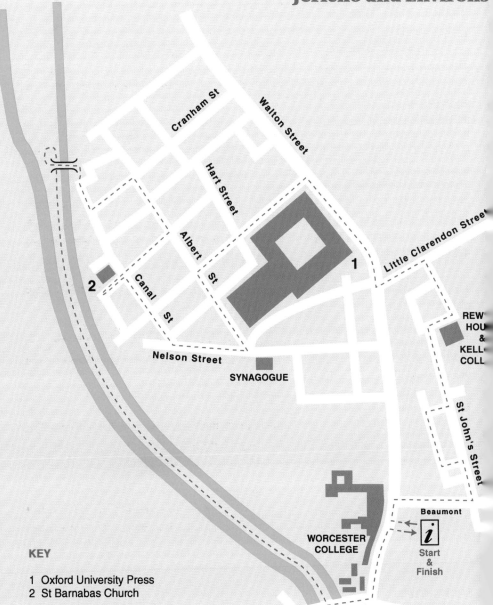

KEY

1 Oxford University Press
2 St Barnabas Church

- - - - - - - - - - Route of the walk

Walk 8
JERICHO AND ENVIRONS

Introduction
Oxford is a vibrant, living city and Jericho, Oxford's first suburb, is a good example of a 'non-university' area of the city. Built during the early and mid 19th century its initial population of mainly general labourers found employment in work generated by the canal which opened in 1790. The arrival of the Jericho Iron and Brass Foundry in 1825 increased employment prospects but it was the building of the Oxford University Press (1826-32) which gave long-term security to the area. For the next 100 years, until the Second World War, most of the working population of Jericho was employed by the Press.

In the 1950's there were plans to raze the area to make way for light industrial units. However, the opposition was so intense these plans were shelved and instead the city council embarked on a policy of rehabilitation and renewal which led to the pleasing mixture of old and new visible today.

This mainly urban walk passes a good cross-section of housing and ends with a pleasant half mile stroll along the canal towpath.

Towards the end of the walk there are steps up to a canal bridge which make it unsuitable for wheelchairs, and after heavy rain, 400 yards of the towpath can become quite muddy underfoot.

Length
This walk of almost two miles, mostly in residential areas, is generally flat and easy, and should take a little over an hour to complete.

Buildings
As the main focus of the walk is concerned with the different types of 19th century housing built in this area of Oxford there are few major university or city buildings along the route. Those seen, however, are both important and interesting and the 'Additional Information' section on *pages 69-70* provides a brief overview of those printed in **bold type**.

Starting Point
This walk starts and finishes at the Tourist Information Centre in Gloucester Green.

The Walk

With your back to the Tourist Information Centre turn right and walk through the bollards, turning right again up Worcester Street. At the traffic lights, with **Worcester College** on your left, cross Beaumont Street and turn right.

Mudscraper - Beaumont Street

After five yards pause to read the inscription on the stone pillar referring to the King's House, **Beaumont Palace**, the birthplace of Richard the Lionheart, before continuing along this street described by Sir Nikolaus Pevsner as 'the finest street ensemble in Oxford'. Built 1823-28 to provide superior housing, most of the buildings are now occupied by dentists, doctors, solicitors, architects and similar professional firms. Reminders of their original purpose, however, can be seen in the several mudscrapers and coal-hole covers which have survived.

Turn left into St John's Street which was positioned here to give a clear view of the Radcliffe Observatory. Unfortunately today only the rooftop globe, supported by Atlas and Hercules, can be seen directly ahead above the intervening buildings. The houses, although part of the same estate as those in Beaumont Street, were not completed until 1835, are not as grand, and the backs are built with cheaper brick.

Take the second left, Beaumont Lane, and then walk along Beaumont Buildings, a peaceful road of artisan houses which complete this first piece of town planning by St John's College, the forerunner of several larger developments on the college's estates in north Oxford.

Beaumont Buildings

Follow the road until it re-emerges in St John's Street and turn left. Many of these houses have been converted into student accommodation and many of those in Wellington Square, at the end of the road, are now offices and annexes of university departments.

On the right hand corner is Rewley House home both to the **Department for Continuing Education** and to **Kellogg College**.

At the end of St John's Street turn right into Wellington Square, walk round two sides of the square and take the exit left of the steps to emerge into lively Little Clarendon Street with its interesting shops, cafes, and bars. The steps lead to the university's main administration offices often referred to as its 'civil service headquarters'.

Little Clarendon Street

Turn left down Little Clarendon Street, at the bottom cross Walton Street by the zebra crossing and then turn right.

After 100 yards on the left is **Oxford University Press** with its imposing original entrance and on the right are the rear buildings of the Radcliffe Infirmary where, in 1941, the world's first injection of penicillin was given.

Take the next left down Great Clarendon Street passing the playing fields of St Barnabas School on the right and the new buildings of Oxford University Press, opened in 1993, on the left. Cross Hart Street to an area of varied house designs resulting both from the involvement of different builders and from the lack of building restraints.

Turn left into Albert Street and cross Wellington Street to reach Nelson Street. The houses in the triangular road system on the left were not built until the 1870's, a generation after the rest of the estate, and are larger than the typical Jericho house. The **synagogue**, rebuilt in 1973, is directly ahead.

Turn right along Nelson Street for 100 yards before turning right again into Canal Street with the tower of St Barnabas church clearly visible ahead on the left.

Take the second left and walk down to **St Barnabas** church which normally has its front door open allowing access to the viewing window in the porch. After viewing the church return up Cardigan Street noticing that the Radcliffe Observatory, seen earlier on this walk, is again visible behind the buildings directly ahead.

St Barnabas Church

At the second street, Albert Street, turn left and take the second left again to walk down Cranham Street leaving the 'Globe' pub on your right. Turn right at the bottom and then left at the bollards to walk up the steps and over the bridge which crosses the canal.

Market Square

Having crossed the canal turn right, to walk under the bridge just crossed, and carry on along the towpath with the canal on the left and Castle Mill Stream on the right. After 400 yards take the left of two bridges and continue along the towpath with the **canal** and its moored longboats on the left, **Isis Lock** on the right, and very soon the steeple of **Nuffield College** clearly visible ahead.

Emerging at Hythe Bridge Street turn left to obtain a good view of Nuffield College diagonally ahead on the right. Walk to the traffic lights, cross the road, turn left and walk 100 yards up Worcester Street to reach the bollards where a right turn will bring you to the Tourist Information Centre and the finish of the walk.

Additional Information

Worcester College *(see also walk 6 page 55)*

The only Oxford college to have a lake in its grounds. Although today its location is fairly central the college was once considered so isolated it was referred to as Botany Bay. Numbered amongst its alumni are the publisher Rupert Murdoch, Henry Kingsley who ran a mile, rode a mile and rowed a mile in less than 15 minutes, and Thomas de Quincey (1785-1859) who not only wrote *'The Confessions of an Opium Eater'* but also failed his degree because he took such a large dose of opium on the first day of the exam that he was unconscious on the second.

Worcester College

Beaumont Palace *(see also walk 6 page 55)*

When in 1318 Edward II gave what was left of Beaumont Palace to the Carmelites they rented their buildings, which were adjacent to Gloucester College, to the Benedictines. Eventually Gloucester College became Worcester College and in this serendipitous way the building across the road is linked to the birthplace of the only king of England born in Oxford.

Department for Continuing Education

The department draws on the resources of Oxford University to provide academic programmes for mature and non-traditional students. More than 450 different programmes are offered including postgraduate, undergraduate and diploma studies. Courses are also offered abroad.

Kellogg College

Founded in 1990 and named Kellogg College in 1994 in recognition of the support given to adult continuing education in Oxford by the W K Kellogg Foundation. The college exists to support the continuing education work of the university and to provide a college base for adult and part-time students.

Oxford University Press *(see also walk 1 Clarendon Building page 12)*

OUP main entrance

Although printing in Oxford began in 1478 the university didn't have a press until 200 years later. Its original aim was to print the manuscripts rotting in various Oxford libraries but by the beginning of the 18th century it had become a two-pronged business covering the 'learned' and the 'bible' press. The enormous success of the bible press in the first half of the 19th century led, in 1830, to relocation into the larger Walton Street premises. The Press is still a department of the university controlled by the body of senior scholars who make up the Delegates of the Press.

Synagogue

After many years of discussion concerning the location and requirements for the new building, and the dismissal of the original architect, the firm of David Stern and Partners was appointed in 1971 to take over the project. Things then moved quickly and by the end of that year design drawings of the new synagogue had been approved and demolition of the old building had begun. The foundation stone for the new synagogue was laid the following year and the new building was consecrated on 28 April 1974.

St Barnabas

Thomas Combe joined Oxford University Press in 1837 and eventually took over its management. Feeling a degree of responsibility for the spiritual welfare of the increasing local population, which was largely employed by the Press, he paid for St Barnabas to be built. His instructions were for a church of 'strength, solidity and thoroughly sound construction', large enough for 1,000 people, with a dignified interior but with nothing wasted on external appearance.

Canal/Isis Lock *(see also walk 6 page 55)*

The canal took 22 years to build and when completed in 1791 had 42 locks, was crossed by 250 bridges and had cost £307,000. Isis Lock was built by Oxford Gaol prisoners in 1796 to link the canal and the Thames.

Nuffield College *(see also walk 6 page 54)*

When Lord Nuffield bought the canal wharf he offered to build a college on part of the land to improve the visual approach to the west side of Oxford. His original intention was a college of Engineering and Accountancy but he was persuaded to change his mind and the college, which specialises in social studies, aims to provide a link between industry and academia.

Merton College and the City Wall (Walk Two)

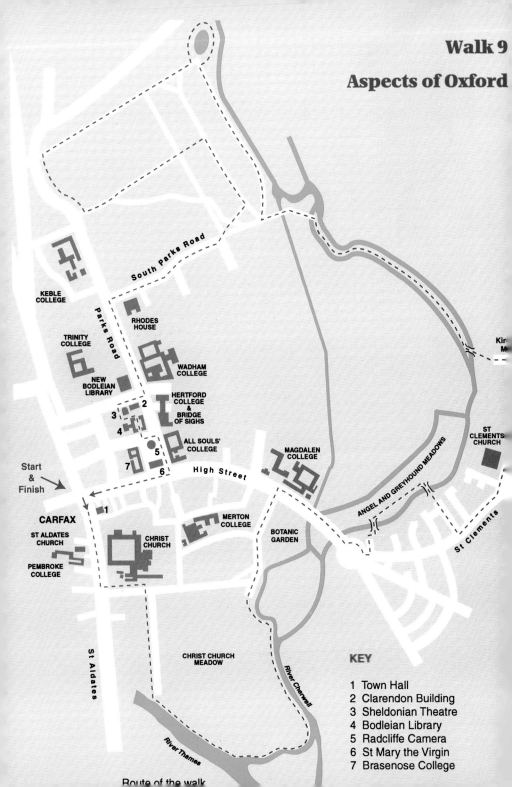

South Parks Road

KEBLE
COLLEGE

Parks Road

RHODES
HOUSE

TRINITY
COLLEGE

WADHAM
COLLEGE

NEW
BODLEIAN
LIBRARY

HERTFORD
COLLEGE
&
BRIDGE
OF SIGHS

2

3

4

ALL SOULS'
COLLEGE

MAGDALEN
COLLEGE

ST
CLEMENTS
CHURCH

5

7

6

High Street

Start
&
Finish

CARFAX

1

MERTON
COLLEGE

BOTANIC
GARDEN

ANGEL AND GREYHOUND MEADOWS

St Clements

ST ALDATES
CHURCH

CHRIST
CHURCH

PEMBROKE
COLLEGE

St Aldates

CHRIST CHURCH
MEADOW

River Cherwell

Kir
M

KEY

1 Town Hall
2 Clarendon Building
3 Sheldonian Theatre
4 Bodleian Library
5 Radcliffe Camera
6 St Mary the Virgin
7 Brasenose College

River Thames

Route of the walk

Walk 9
ASPECTS OF OXFORD

Introduction
There are many differing aspects to Oxford - town and gown, rivers and streams, parks and countryside - and the walks in this book try to give a flavour of that diversity. To enable the visitor, and indeed the local resident, to satisfy particular interests, most of the walks are quite short, take relatively little time to complete and highlight just one aspect of this rather special city.

This walk is different and aims to give an overview of many of the contrasting aspects to be found within a short distance of the city centre. It does this by linking together parts of three of the walks to provide a longer excursion for those with the time and energy to complete it. The links are interesting in themselves and greatly add to the enjoyment of the walk.

Length
The walk, along riverbanks, through streets and meadows, in the Parks and town, is five miles long and takes about three hours to complete. It is flat, easy walking on good firm paths or pavements. Unfortunately two swinging 'kissing type' gates make it unsuitable for wheelchairs.

Buildings
To ensure directions are clear and straightforward minimal information is included in the walk description on the buildings seen. However, the 'Additional Information' section on *pages 81-86* provides a brief overview of each of the locations printed in **bold type**.

Starting Point
This circular walk starts and finishes in Carfax in the centre of Oxford.

Descriptions
Much of this walk comprises sections from *walks 1, 2 and 7*. Both the walk description and the additional information comments for these sections are repeated here to ensure clarity and to prevent overcomplication.

The Walk

Cardinal's hat

From Carfax walk south down the left hand side of St Aldates passing after a few yards the **Town Hall** and the Museum of Oxford, with **Tom Tower** the imposing bell tower of **Christ Church** clearly visible ahead. A little further, as you pass Christ Church, notice the cardinals' hats carved on the towers, a reminder of the college's founder, Cardinal Wolsey. Also look through the main gate of Christ Church at Tom Quad, the largest quad in Oxford, with a lead copy of Giovanni da Bologna's *Mercury* in the centre. Across the road on the right is **Pembroke College** with its entrance tucked away beyond St Aldate's church.

To avoid 6 steps in the War Memorial Garden skip the rest of this page and go to the paragraph on the next page headed 'Alternative Route To Avoid 6 Steps'

Continue past a garage entrance and about 100 yards after Christ Church turn left through imposing wrought iron gates into the **War Memorial Garden**. Notice the sword inlaid into the paving at the entrance with an inscription from John Bunyan's *Pilgrims Progress* 'My sword I give to him that shall succeed me in my pilgrimage'.

Christ Church from the Memorial Garden

Walk 5 or 6 paces into the Garden and pause to look at some of the buildings. On the left is Christ Church with Tom Tower and the Hall in full view, on the right is the north wing of the Faculty of Music containing the Bate Collection of English and European woodwind, brass and percussion instruments. Behind, across the road, is Alice's Shop where Alice of *Alice in Wonderland* and *Alice through the Looking Glass* bought her sweets. Alice in real life was Alice Liddell the daughter of the Dean of Christ Church.

Walk through the Garden, up two sets of three steps each, into **Christ Church Meadow**.

Alternative Route To Avoid 6 Steps

Immediately after Christ Church there is an entrance on the left with a notice *Entrance to Garages Do Not Obstruct.* Turn left through this entrance and after 100 yards turn left again. After a further 50 yards rejoin the main walk opposite the visitors entrance to Christ Church.

The diversion to avoid the steps rejoins the main walk at this point.

After a few yards, opposite the visitors entrance to Christ Church, turn right along Poplar Walk which was planted in 1872 by Alice's father Dean Liddell. Continue between the trees, along this very pleasant stretch of meadow which often has contented cattle grazing on your left, and after a quarter of a mile reach the River Thames or Isis as it is known hereabouts.

Turn left and walk along the side of the river stopping if you wish to sit and refresh mind, body or both at one of the many convenient benches along the way.

After 300 yards ignore the bridge on your right and continue straight ahead keeping to the pathway. The walk now follows a delightful, slow running link between the two rivers of Oxford, the Isis and the Cherwell, a little known but idyllic stretch of water for **punting**.

A further half mile brings you to a fork in the river and the pathway follows the left fork. Clearly visible over to the right, behind the trees, is **Magdalen College** Tower where from the top at dawn every May Day morning the choir sings an invocation to summer whilst several thousand people dance and make merry in the street below.

Continue ahead, ignoring after 200 yards the major path, Broad Walk, which joins from the left, and keep right reaching after a further 100 yards the railings of the **Botanic Garden**. Continue along this path with the railings on your right.

Botanic Garden View

Leave the Parks through the gates, walk up Rose Lane, cross the High Street and turn right to walk past Magdalen College and its tower. Walk over **Magdalen Bridge** and at the roundabout with the **Victoria Fountain** keep left up St Clement's Street.

Occasionally after prolonged rain Angel and Greyhound Meadows flood. If this is the case ignore the following two paragraphs.

Take the first left to walk down York Place turning right at the stream. Keep to the path which goes into a car park for 20 yards before turning left over the bridge to enter Angel Meadow.

Turn right and walk along a tree-lined pathway before emerging into the meadow, cross with the path into Greyhound Meadow and after a further 40 yards turn right over a bridge walking to the top of Bath Street to rejoin St Clement's Street. Turn left.

Victoria Fountain

At this point the main walk and the alternative rejoin

Continue along St Clement's Street to the main junction and at the traffic lights bear left along Marston Road soon passing **St Clement's Church** on the left. Walk 400 yards up this gently inclining road with a stone wall on the left. Immediately at the end of the wall turn left down a lane with Magdalen College playing fields over the hedge on the right.

At the end of the lane walk over the bridge into the Parks and keep on this pathway, **Mesopotamia**, for the next half mile crossing two bridges and ignoring another two on the right. After half a mile as the path swings left, cross the bridge, turn right, go through the gates and turn left along a path over another bridge keeping the railings on your left.

Immediately after crossing the bridge turn right through the gates and take the right fork keeping the river Cherwell on your right. Continue alongside this stretch of the river which is very popular for punting, and pass a bridge to reach a large lily pond, built in 1925 and now home to several varieties of waterfowl.

Punting on the Cherwell

Keeping the pond on your left walk around it until the path swings right, away from the pond, near a seat dedicated to the memory of John St L Philpot. Keep to the path and continue straight ahead ignoring all other paths joining from both left and right but noticing, after a short while, the **university cricket ground** on the left.

After a third of a mile, 20 yards before the gate leading out of the Parks, turn left with the path which swings in a wide arc with the uninspiring, functional buildings of the Science Triangle visible across the road.

At the next path junction, with the chapel of **Keble College** clearly visible diagonally right, turn left and after 20 yards keep to the left fork and walk straight ahead for a quarter of a mile.

Keble College Chapel

After passing the back of the cricket pavilion a crossing of the paths is reached 50 yards before a bridge spanning the river. Turn right to pass, on the right, a seat dedicated to the memory of Peter Hancock, and continue for 300 yards before taking the right fork, through the bollards and then past South Lodge to the exit gate. Walk through the gate and turn right along South Parks Road.

On the left is the stark 1960's concrete building of the Department of Zoology and Psychology designed by Sir Leslie Martin. Walk for 100 yards to the traffic lights, cross the road and continue ahead passing the functional buildings of the science area which lie across the road.

Pass **Rhodes House** on the left and the Inorganic Chemistry building on the right to reach the end of South Parks Road then turn left into Parks Road. After 200 yards reach the much photographed blue wrought iron gates and garden quad of **Trinity College** and a little further on the left, **Wadham College**, used in the filming of *'Brideshead Revisited'*. With the **New Bodleian Library** across the road on the right continue to the traffic lights and cross over Holywell Street.

The Sheldonian through the Bridge of Sighs

On Saturday afternoons and Sundays skip the next two pages and go to the section of the walk description headed 'Saturday pm and Sunday Alternative' on page 81

Turn right again to cross into Broad Street, walk past the Clarendon Building steps and walk up the second set of steps leading to the Sheldonian Theatre.

Walk to the right keeping the **Sheldonian Theatre** designed by Christopher Wren on your left to arrive in a courtyard with the Sheldonian on your left and the 15th century **Divinity School** on your right.

Hertford College

Continue to an open gravelled courtyard with, on your left, the **Clarendon Building** with its rooftop statues representing the nine muses, and visible ahead across the road, the **Bridge of Sighs** linking the two buildings of **Hertford College**.

Turn right opposite the Clarendon through an opening which leads to **Schools Quad** now part of the **Bodleian Library** but originally built as lecture rooms and libraries.

Through the door behind the statue of the Earl of Pembroke enter the Divinity School.

On leaving the Divinity School exit Schools Quad on the right between the 'Schola Musicae' and the 'Schola Naturalis Philosophiae' to the stunning Radcliffe Square.

Directly ahead dominating the square is the **Radcliffe Camera** with its original ground floor arcade now enclosed to form part of the building; to the right is **Brasenose College** and to the left **All Souls College**.

Walk to the left keeping the Radcliffe Camera on your right and take a moment to look through the gates at the Great Quad of All Souls designed by Nicholas Hawksmoor and built in the first quarter of the 18th century. On the north side is a sundial designed by Christopher Wren when he was the college bursar.

Oriel College

Ahead is the university church of **St Mary the Virgin**. For a small charge it is possible to climb the 127 steps of the tower and to be rewarded with probably the most breathtaking views of anywhere in Oxford.

Enter St Mary the Virgin through the tower door and walk through the gift shop into the church. Exit diagonally opposite at the back of the church into the High Street facing the north side of Oriel College with a statue of Cecil Rhodes towards the top of the tower. This is the only statue in Oxford of a man dressed in civilian as opposed to clerical or military clothes.

Turn right and walk along The High, past Brasenose College on the right, to the finishing point at Carfax.

The Clarendon from the Bridge of Sighs

After a few yards reach on the left the **Bridge of Sighs** linking the two buildings of **Hertford College**. On the right the Sheldonian and the Clarendon can be seen from a different perspective.

A few yards further opposite the main entrance to Hertford College is the entrance to **Schools Quad** now part of the **Bodleian Library** but originally built as lecture rooms and libraries. The crests on the entrance doors are of the 20 colleges in existence in 1620 when the Quad was built.

Continue down Catte Street to reach the stunning Radcliffe Square. Directly ahead dominating the square is the **Radcliffe Camera** with its original ground floor arcade now enclosed to form part of the building; to the right is **Brasenose College** and to the left **All Souls College**.

All Souls College Gates

Walk to the left keeping the Radcliffe Camera on your right and take a moment to look through the gates at the Great Quad of All Souls designed by Nicholas Hawksmoor and built in the first quarter of the 18th century. On the north side is a sundial designed by Christopher Wren when he was the college bursar. Ahead is the university church of **St Mary the Virgin**. For a small charge it is possible to climb the 127 steps of the tower and to be rewarded with probably the most breathtaking views of anywhere in Oxford.

Enter St Mary the Virgin through the tower door and walk through the gift shop into the church. Exit diagonally opposite at the back of the church into the High Street facing the north side of Oriel College with a statue of Cecil Rhodes towards the top of the tower. This is the only statue in Oxford of a man dressed in civilian as opposed to clerical or military clothes.

Turn right and walk along The High, past Brasenose College on the right, to the finishing point at Carfax.

Additional Information

Town Hall

Opened by the Prince of Wales, later Edward VII, on 12 May 1897. The results of parliamentary elections are announced from the balcony over the entrance and on the roof is a weather vane featuring a golden ox from the city's coat-of-arms. On the south corner is the Museum of Oxford.

Tom Tower

Designed by Christopher Wren and built in 1682 above Wolsey's 1527 archway and turrets. Inside the tower is Great Tom, the loudest bell in Oxford, which chimes 101 times every evening at 9.05pm to recall the 101 students resident in 1682 and their curfew time of 9pm. However, as Great Tom keeps local time not GMT and since the city is 5 minutes west of Greenwich, the bell chimes at 9.05pm!

Town Hall

Christ Church *(see also walk 3 page 26)*

Founded as Cardinal College in 1525 by Cardinal Wolsey but unfinished when he fell from power, the college was refounded as Christ Church in 1545 by Henry VIII. Perhaps the grandest of Oxford colleges it numbers amongst its alumnae 14 Prime Ministers, John Wesley the founder of Methodism, and William Penn the founder of Pennsylvania. The college chapel is also the cathedral of the Oxford diocese.

Pembroke College

Founded in 1624 and named after the University Chancellor the 3rd Earl of Pembroke, the south side of the college incorporates a long stretch of the old city wall. Samuel Johnson, compiler of the dictionary and a student at Pembroke, complained when fined for skipping a lecture that he had 'been fined tuppence for a lecture that was not worth a penny'. Another student James Smithson left his fortune to the United States government who used it to found the Smithsonian Institute.

James Smithson Memorial Plaque (inside college)

War Memorial Garden

Laid out in 1925 the garden commemorates all Oxford people, whether from the city or the university, who died in the First World War.

Christ Church Meadow

Part of the meadow was a gift from Lady Montacute who in 1454 was buried in the priory of St Frideswide: the priory was subsequently incorporated into the college chapel during the building of Christ Church. It is difficult to believe that during the 1950's and 1960's various schemes were put forward to build a road through the meadow and only intense opposition resulted in the plans finally being shelved in 1966.

Punting

Punting

The word 'punt' first appeared in written English about AD1000 and meant any small craft. Nowadays it is a long, narrow, flat bottomed boat propelled by pushing a pole against the bottom of the river. Sounds simple but watching some people's attempts can be an enjoyable and hilarious experience!

Magdalen College *(see also walk 5 page 46)*

Pronounced 'Maudlin' and founded by William of Waynflete during the Wars of the Roses in 1458 it has 100 acres of grounds, more than a mile of riverside walks and a herd of deer. The 144 ft high tower was used as an observation post during the Civil War and was stocked with missiles to be used if Cromwell's forces attempted to march over the bridge. Edward Gibbon of *Decline & Fall of the Roman Empire* fame described his 14 months here as 'the most idle and unprofitable of my whole life'.

Botanic Garden

Founded in 1621 as a Physic Garden to provide medicinal herbs it has evolved into a collection of over 8,000 plants in a compact, beautifully laid out setting accurately reflecting the appearance of a Tudor or Stuart college garden.

Magdalen Bridge

Magdalen Bridge

Built in 1772-78 and widened in 1835 and again in 1882 this is the latest in a long line of bridges, dating back to at least 1004, which have crossed the river at this point. It has on many occasions been the official welcoming or departure spot for important visitors including Queen Elizabeth I who took her official leave of the city from the bridge in 1566.

Victoria Fountain

Built, two years late in 1899, as a tribute to Queen Victoria for her Diamond Jubilee on the site of the old toll house for the bridge.

St Clement's Church

The original church was on the Plain (as is the Victoria Fountain) but moved to its present location in 1826 when a larger building was required. The three bells were brought from the old church and one, cast in the 13th century, is the oldest bell in Oxford.

Mesopotamia

The name comes from the Greek meaning 'between two rivers' and is Oxford's version of the original between the Euphrates and the Tigres in what is now Iraq.

University Cricket Ground

Opened in 1881 the ground is one of the few in the country where first class cricket can be watched free of charge. The pavilion, designed by T G Jackson, was built in 1880.

Mesopotamia View

Keble College *(see also walk 5 page 44)*

The chapel, which was paid for by William Gibbs who had made his fortune selling guano, was opened in 1876. It was never consecrated because this would have involved the participation of the Bishop of Oxford who was deeply mistrusted by the college Council.

Rhodes House *(see also walk 5 page 44)*

Rhodes scholarships, which are normally held for two years, are open to both men and women between the ages of 19 and 25. Nearly 100 selection committees throughout the world select scholars on the basis of academic record, confidential testimonials and personal interview.

Trinity College
(see also walks 1 and 5 pages 11 and 45)

Trinity is set back on all sides, including its Broad Street frontage, and although close to the centre of the city is the most secluded of the old colleges. Terence Rattigan, the playwright, was a student here but never graduated saying he didn't want to be 'marked out for life by getting a degree'. The explorer Richard Burton on the other hand was rusticated (temporarily expelled) and confident that his family didn't know the meaning of the word explained he had been given an extra holiday because he had taken a double first.

Trinity College - Front Quad

Wadham College *(see also walk 5 page 45)*
'Breakfast Meetings' conjure up visions of high powered executives solving major problems early in the morning, but a breakfasting club founded in 1842 had altogether different objectives. The decisions of the Wadham Beefsteak Club whose aim was to foster *'good fellowship by periodical meetings at breakfast'* majored on food. Initially only beefsteak and sausages could be served, but after much discussion and deep thought it was decided, three years later, that if sausages were out of season kidneys could be substituted. Mutton chops, however, never received the seal of approval.

New Bodleian Broad Street entrance

New Bodleian Library *(see also walk 5 page 45)*
In 1610 Thomas Bodley who refounded the university library which now bears his name, came to an agreement with the Stationers Office giving the Bodleian the right to a free copy of every book registered at Stationers Hall. As a result each week a large lorry delivers a free copy of every book published in this country during the previous week. There are four other 'copyright' libraries enjoying the same privilege: the British Library, the national libraries of Scotland and of Wales, and Cambridge University library.

Sheldonian Theatre *(see also walk 7 page 60)*
Built 1664-69 this is the first major building designed by Sir Christopher Wren who at the time was only 31 and was Professor of Astronomy! The design is based on the Marcellus Theatre in Rome and the theatre is named after Archbishop Sheldon, University Chancellor and Archbishop of Canterbury, who footed the bill. The 'Emperors Heads' on the Broad Street side of the building simply mark the northern boundary and, although visually attractive, are of no other significance.

Divinity School
This is the oldest university as opposed to college building in Oxford. Built 1420-1483 the initials or coat of arms of those who contributed to the cost are carved on the bosses of the magnificent ceiling. Initially the building was for lectures and examinations in Divinity but it now forms part of the Bodleian Library.

Clarendon Building *(see also walk 8 Oxford University Press page 70)*
Designed by Nicholas Hawksmoor, a pupil of Wren, and built in 1712 by the Oxford University Press for their printing works which had outgrown previous premises in the Sheldonian Theatre. The building is now part of the Bodleian

Library and the Press is in modern buildings a mile away. However, a felicitous reminder of its former activities is the 'Clarendon Press' imprint on all OUP books.

Bridge of Sighs *(see also walk 5 page 47)*
One of the most frequently photographed and well known landmarks in Oxford and familiarly named after the Ponte dei Sospiri in Venice. The bridge, built 1913-14, links the two buildings of Hertford College.

Hertford College
Hertford has had a very chequered and unusual existence. It's history goes back to the foundation of Hart Hall in 1284 and during the next 600 years, culminating in its refoundation in 1874, it was twice an academic hall and twice a college. Evelyn Waugh, an undergraduate here, portrayed Oxford life in the 1920's as he saw it in his novel 'Brideshead Revisited' a portrait of an Oxford now long gone.

Schools Quad
'Schools' in this context means 'teaching rooms' and the quad was built 1613-24 to bring together the lecture rooms until then dispersed throughout the city. Teaching in those days was in Latin and over the doors, in Latin, can still be seen the early 17th century curriculum. The statue is of the 3rd Earl of Pembroke, Chancellor of the University when the quad was built and the man to whom Shakespeare dedicated his first folio. Schools Quad is now part of the Bodleian Library.

17th Century Lecture Room - Schools Quad

Bodleian Library
The main research library of the University, founded by Sir Thomas Bodley and opened in 1602. Today it is housed in several buildings and contains nearly 7 million books, more than 1 million maps and has more than 160 kilometres of shelving. It is not a lending library and even Charles I, when he was resident in Oxford during the Civil War, was refused permission to borrow a book.

Radcliffe Camera
John Radcliffe who studied at Oxford and later became physician to the joint monarchs William and Mary left much of his wealth and all of his medical books to the university. More than 20 years later in 1737, after the site had finally been cleared, building work started on this first round library in Britain. In 1860 it became part of the Bodleian Library and is now reading rooms mainly used by undergraduates.

Brasenose College *(see also walk 3 page 28)*
Founded in 1509 and named after the 'brazen nose' 13th century door-knocker which students took with them to Stamford in Lincolnshire in 1333 when they left the then turbulent situation in Oxford for a calmer environment. In 1890 the college bought a complete house so they could get the knocker back! It now has prime position above the Principle's place at High Table.

All Souls College *(see also walk 3 page 28)*
A unique college which takes neither undergraduate nor graduate students, only research Fellows. The first female Fellow, Susan Hurley of Santa Barbara, California was elected in 1981. Founded in 1438 as a memorial to those who died in the 100 Years War with France its full name is The College of All Souls of the Faithful Departed.

St Mary the Virgin *(see also walk 3 page 28)*
Although mentioned in the Domesday Book of 1086 the oldest parts of the church we now see, the last in a series built on the same site, are the 13th century tower and 14th century spire. The university developed in the area of the church and until specialised university buildings were available, St Mary's was used for university meetings, examinations and ceremonies. Indeed the flat roofed extension which is now a cafe was once the university parliament building.

INDEX

Market Deliveries

88